W9-CDF-126

HEART OF DARKNESS

OTHER TITLES IN THE GREENHAVEN PRESS LITERARY COMPANION SERIES:

AMERICAN AUTHORS

Maya Angelou
Stephen Crane
Emily Dickinson
William Faulkner
F. Scott Fitzgerald
Robert Frost
Nathaniel Hawthorne
Ernest Hemingway
Herman Melville
Arthur Miller
Eugene O'Neill
Edgar Allan Poe
John Steinbeck
Mark Twain
Walt Whitman
Thornton Wilder

AMERICAN LITERATURE

The Adventures of
  Huckleberry Finn
The Adventures of Tom
  Sawyer
The Call of the Wild
The Catcher in the Rye
The Crucible
Death of a Salesman
The Glass Menagerie
The Grapes of Wrath
The Great Gatsby
Of Mice and Men
The Old Man and the Sea
The Pearl
The Scarlet Letter
A Separate Peace

BRITISH AUTHORS

Jane Austen
Joseph Conrad
Charles Dickens

BRITISH LITERATURE

Animal Farm
Beowulf
Brave New World
The Canterbury Tales
Great Expectations
Hamlet
Julius Caesar
Lord of the Flies
Macbeth
Pride and Prejudice
Romeo and Juliet
Shakespeare: The Comedies
Shakespeare: The Histories
Shakespeare: The Sonnets
Shakespeare: The Tragedies
A Tale of Two Cities
Wuthering Heights

WORLD AUTHORS

Fyodor Dostoyevsky
Homer
Sophocles

WORLD LITERATURE

All Quiet on the Western
  Front
Antigone
The Diary of a Young Girl
A Doll's House

THE GREENHAVEN PRESS
Literary Companion
TO BRITISH LITERATURE

READINGS ON

HEART OF DARKNESS

Clarice Swisher, *Book Editor*

David L. Bender, *Publisher*
Bruno Leone, *Executive Editor*
Bonnie Szumski, *Series Editor*

Greenhaven Press, Inc., San Diego, CA

T/4376

Every effort has been made to trace the owners of copyrighted material. The articles in this volume may have been edited for content, length, and/or reading level. The titles have been changed to enhance the editorial purpose. Those interested in locating the original source will find the complete citation on the first page of each article.

Library of Congress Cataloging-in-Publication Data

Readings on Heart of darkness / editor, Clarice Swisher.
        p.   cm. — (Greenhaven Press literary companion
   to British literature)
     Includes bibliographical references and index.
     ISBN 1-56510-822-1 (pbk. : alk. paper).—
   ISBN 1-56510-823-X (lib. : alk. paper)
     1. Conrad, Joseph, 1857–1924. Heart of darkness.
   2. Psychological fiction, English—History and criticism.
   3. Africa—In literature. I. Swisher, Clarice, 1933–   .
   II. Title: Heart of darkness. III. Series.
   PR6005.04H4779   1999
   823'.912—dc21   98-48268
                                                                CIP

Cover photo: Photofest

San Diego, CA 92198-9009
Printed in the U.S.A.

"... and the tranquil waterway leading to the uttermost ends of the earth flowed somber under an overcast sky—seemed to lead into the heart of an immense darkness."

—Joseph Conrad, *Heart of Darkness*

CONTENTS

Chapter 1: Major Themes in *Heart of Darkness*

Chapter 2: Kurtz and Marlow

Chapter 3: Conrad's Style and Methods

dominate inferior primitive peoples. *Heart of Darkness* exposes the errors in these popular beliefs.

FOREWORD

*"'Tis the good reader that
makes the good book."*

Ralph Waldo Emerson

The story's bare facts are simple: The captain, an old and scarred seafarer, walks with a peg leg made of whale ivory. He relentlessly drives his crew to hunt the world's oceans for the great white whale that crippled him. After a long search, the ship encounters the whale and a fierce battle ensues. Finally the captain drives his harpoon into the whale, but the harpoon line catches the captain about the neck and drags him to his death.

A simple story, a straightforward plot—yet, since the 1851 publication of Herman Melville's *Moby-Dick*, readers and critics have found many meanings in the struggle between Captain Ahab and the whale. To some, the novel is a cautionary tale that depicts how Ahab's obsession with revenge leads to his insanity and death. Others believe that the whale represents the unknowable secrets of the universe and that Ahab is a tragic hero who dares to challenge fate by attempting to discover this knowledge. Perhaps Melville intended Ahab as a criticism of Americans' tendency to become involved in well-intentioned but irrational causes. Or did Melville model Ahab after himself, letting his fictional character express his anger at what he perceived as a cruel and distant god?

Although literary critics disagree over the meaning of *Moby-Dick*, readers do not need to choose one particular interpretation in order to gain an understanding of Melville's novel. Instead, by examining various analyses, they can gain numerous insights into the issues that lie under the surface of the basic plot. Studying the writings of literary critics can also aid readers in making their own assessments of *Moby-Dick* and other literary works and in developing analytical thinking skills.

The Greenhaven Literary Companion Series was created with these goals in mind. Designed for young adults, this unique anthology series provides an engaging and comprehensive introduction to literary analysis and criticism. The essays included in the Literary Companion Series are chosen for their accessibility to a young adult audience and are expertly edited in consideration of both the reading and comprehension levels of this audience. In addition, each essay is introduced by a concise summation that presents the contributing writer's main themes and insights. Every anthology in the Literary Companion Series contains a varied selection of critical essays that cover a wide time span and express diverse views. Wherever possible, primary sources are represented through excerpts from authors' notebooks, letters, and journals and through contemporary criticism.

Each title in the Literary Companion Series pays careful consideration to the historical context of the particular author or literary work. In-depth biographies and detailed chronologies reveal important aspects of authors' lives and emphasize the historical events and social milieu that influenced their writings. To facilitate further research, every anthology includes primary and secondary source bibliographies of articles and/or books selected for their suitability for young adults. These engaging features make the Greenhaven Literary Companion series ideal for introducing students to literary analysis in the classroom or as a library resource for young adults researching the world's great authors and literature.

Exceptional in its focus on young adults, the Greenhaven Literary Companion Series strives to present literary criticism in a compelling and accessible format. Every title in the series is intended to spark readers' interest in leading American and world authors, to help them broaden their understanding of literature, and to encourage them to formulate their own analyses of the literary works that they read. It is the editors' hope that young adult readers will find these anthologies to be true companions in their study of literature.

INTRODUCTION

Joseph Conrad's *Heart of Darkness* is a difficult book with no clear, single interpretation. In their attempts to understand it, readers have asked questions on four topics.

1. What is the significance of the journey? What does a "heart of darkness" mean?

2. Is the book about Kurtz or Marlow? What does Kurtz represent? Why does Kurtz die and Marlow live? Why does Marlow lie?

3. Who is the narrator? Why is the story so hard to follow? Why does the book read so slowly? Why is this novel considered good literature?

4. Is Conrad really describing Africa at the end of the nineteenth century? Is he accurate about the practices of colonialism or is he exaggerating?

Readings on Heart of Darkness devotes a chapter to each of these topics, providing readers with many critical voices. In some chapters critics have opposing views. These critical essays will guide the reader through this complex novel and provide ideas and interpretations.

This volume comprises a variety of criticism written by many of the most well-respected Conrad critics. It includes essays by Albert J. Guerard, Frederick R. Karl, Ian Watt, J.I.M. Stewart, Jeremy Hawthorn, and Cedric Watts. A novelist from Nigeria offers a modern third world opinion of Conrad's views.

Readings on Heart of Darkness includes many special features that make research and literary criticism accessible and understandable. A biography of Joseph Conrad recounts important events and people in his life. An annotated table of contents lets readers quickly preview the contents of individual essays. A chronology features a list of significant events in Conrad's life placed in a broader historical context. Bibliographies include other books by Conrad, books on Conrad's time, and additional critical sources suitable for further research.

Each essay has aids for clear understanding. Individual introductions serve to explain the main points, which are then identified by subheads within the essays. Footnotes explain uncommon references and define unfamiliar words. Taken together, these aids make the Greenhaven Press *Literary Companion Series* an indispensable research tool.

Joseph Conrad: A Biography

"I am another kind of person," Joseph Conrad wrote to his agent. Though Conrad was responding to a particular misunderstanding, the line characterizes Conrad professionally and personally. Conrad, an orphan by age eleven, grew up in Poland speaking Polish, yet became a major British novelist and short story writer who wrote all his works in English. For fifteen years, he worked on British merchant ships before becoming a writer. He wrote romantic stories energized with adventure. "I am modern," he repeated to those who misjudged his work.

Jozef Teodor Konrad Nalecz Korzeniowski was born on December 3, 1857, in Berdichev in the Polish Ukraine, a hundred miles southwest of Kiev. His father, Apollo Korzeniowski, educated in Oriental languages, law, and literature at St. Petersburg University, was a writer and translator. As a Polish patriot, Apollo believed in sacrifice for one's country and led others in political causes. Conrad's mother, Ewelina Bobrowska, called Eva, thirteen years younger than Apollo, was a warm, imaginative woman who loved Apollo and chose him in spite of her parents' disapproval. Both Eva and Apollo were members of the *szlachta*, the ruling class. While Eva's father ignored politics and focused his attention on increasing his wealth, the Korzeniowskis devoted time, energy, and money to the revolutionary cause.

Conrad's Disrupted Childhood

Apollo's political activities profoundly affected Conrad's childhood. In 1795 Poland's neighbors, threatened by Poland's liberal constitution, partitioned the country. Russia annexed the central and eastern territory; Poland retained the western part until 1830, when Prussia acquired it; and the southern part was incorporated into the Austrian Empire. When Napoleon invaded Russia in the early 1800s, Poles expected reunification, but the division remained. After two

14

failed revolutions in 1830 and 1846, another uprising was brewing in the early 1860s. Apollo, who resisted oppressive Russian rule and provoked authorities by his dress and his radical agitation for resistance, was arrested and imprisoned for seven months. While he awaited trial, Eva took Conrad, age three, to see his father through the prison window. Apollo was found guilty and exiled; Eva and Conrad traveled with him to Vologda, 250 miles north of Moscow, where they survived the cold winter on meager rations. From this experience, all three of them became sick; Eva developed tuberculosis and died on April 18, 1865, when Conrad was seven. He was devastated by his mother's death, and Apollo assumed guilt for his arrest, their exile, and the death of his wife. Conrad, a frail child, became nervous and unstable and often ill; his unhealthy state continued into adult life.

After Eva's death, Conrad lived in lonely, sad isolation with Apollo, who had also contracted tuberculosis. Aside from a brief stay with his grandmother in Kiev to recuperate from illness, Conrad took care of his sick father. Because Apollo wanted nothing of the hated Russians and their culture to influence his son, he kept him out of school and away from other children and taught Conrad himself. To escape loneliness and the stress of his demanding father's instruction, Conrad immersed himself in reading. Apollo wrote of his son:

> Poor child: he does not know what a contemporary playmate is; he looks at the decrepitude of my sadness and who knows if that sight does not make his young heart wrinkled or his awakening soul grizzled. These are important reasons for forcing me to tear the poor child away from my dejected heart. . . .

> Since last autumn my health has been declining badly and my dear little mite takes care of me. . . .

> My life is, at present, confined solely to Konradek. I teach him all I know myself—alas, it is not much; I guard him against the influence of the local atmosphere and the little mite is growing up as though in a cloister.

Prince Galitzen, the governor of Chernikhov, saw that Apollo was dying after five and a half years in Russia, and no longer a threat to the government. Released, father and son moved to Lvov and then to Kraków in southern Poland. By this time, Apollo's health had worsened; he said to a friend, "I am broken, fit for nothing, too tired even to spit upon things." Conrad watched his father's slow decline from tuberculosis until May 13, 1869, when Apollo died. His funeral brought out several thousand patriotic Poles whom eleven-year-old Conrad led in a procession through the streets to the burial site. In *Joseph Conrad: A Biography,* Jeffrey Meyers describes the role model Apollo had provided for his son as "a volatile temperament, an anguished patriotism, the bitterness of shattered hopes, the trauma of defeat and a deep-rooted pessimism." Thirty years later, however, Conrad remembered his father more generously:

> A man of great sensibilities; of exalted and dreamy temperament; with a terrible gift of irony and of gloomy disposition; withal of strong religious feelings degenerating after the loss of his wife into mysticism touched with despair. His aspect was distinguished; his conversation very fascinating; his face in repose somber, lighted all over when he [rarely] smiled. I remember him well. For the last two years of his life I lived alone with him.

Conrad the orphan was placed under the guardianship of his doting grandmother Theophila Bobrowska and his uncle Count Ladislaw Mniszek, but it was Conrad's uncle Thaddeus, Eva's widowed brother, who took over full responsibility for his nephew. He sent Conrad to a small school run by Mr. Louis Georgeon in Kraków. During the summer of 1870, Thaddeus hired Adam Pulman to tutor Conrad in Latin and German so that he could enter St. Jacek's gymnasium, but Conrad lacked the discipline to meet the rigorous curriculum. In *Joseph Conrad: A Critical Biography,* Jocelyn Baines explains Conrad's poor school performance:

> Conrad seems to have disliked school-life, and it is not surprising, in view of his unorthodox upbringing, that he should have found the unaccustomed discipline of regular work irksome. It is probable, too, that academically he was by temperament lazy. . . . Apollo had earlier found that he "showed no love of study." Apparently he liked always to be untrammelled, and at school or at home preferred to lounge rather than sit.

Thaddeus then sent the fifteen-year-old Conrad to a boarding house for orphans of the 1863 insurrection, a place run by a distant cousin Antony Syroczynski. There Conrad had friends his own age and fell in love. Conrad later wrote about his first loves in *The Arrow of Gold.*

During this period Conrad determined to go to sea. His romantic longing for the sea grew out of his boyhood reading of sea adventures, including those by Victor Hugo, James Fenimore Cooper, and Frederick Marryat. Conrad also loved geography and studied it at the expense of his school subjects, once pointing at the Congo saying he wanted to go there. Moreover, he wanted to leave Poland. The relatives finally consented to allow him to join the French merchant navy, and Conrad at seventeen left on a train for the Mediterranean French seaport of Marseilles in October 1874.

CONRAD'S FRENCH EXPERIENCES

Conrad's uncle Thaddeus gave Conrad an allowance and arranged contacts in Marseilles who offered him a social life as well as a job. The ship-owning family the Delestangs included Conrad in their cultural events and introduced him to artists and intellectuals who became his friends. Baptistin, a cousin of the Delestangs, explored the night life of the city with Conrad and brought him to the harbor where he developed friendships with the seamen who worked on pilot boats guiding ships into harbor. The sailors invited Conrad to join them on their boats at any time, night or day; he wrote in his memoirs:

> The very first whole day I ever spent on salt water was by invitation, in a big half-decked pilot-boat, cruising under close reefs on the lookout, in misty, blowing weather, for the sails of ships and the smoke of steamers rising out there, beyond the slim and tall Planier lighthouse cutting the line of the wind-swept horizon with a white perpendicular stroke. They were hospitable souls, these sturdy Provencal seamen.

Two months after arriving in Marseilles, Conrad made the first of three voyages on ships owned by the Delestangs. First as a passenger on the *Mont Blanc,* Conrad sailed on December 11, 1874, to Martinique in the Caribbean. Near the Straits of Gibraltar he experienced his first storm; in *The Mirror of the Sea,* Conrad describes his reaction: "The very first Christmas night I ever spent away from land was employed in running before a Gulf of Lyons gale, which made the old ship groan in every timber. . . . I listened for the first time with the curiosity of my tender years to the song of the wind in the ship's rigging." On his second voyage on the *Mont Blanc* to Martinique in 1875, Conrad served as an apprentice seaman. On the return voyage stormy weather damaged the ship, requiring it to be repaired in Le Havre, France. Rather than wait, Conrad left the ship, took a train to Paris and then to Marseilles, and lost his trunk along the way. In 1876 on a larger ship, the *Saint Antoine,* Conrad served as a steward, earning thirty-five francs a month. Besides Martinique, the *Saint Antoine* docked in Colombia, Venezuela, St. Thomas, and Haiti, giving Conrad glimpses of South America that he would use as the setting for *Nostromo*. He also met first mate Dominic Cervone, who became the model for major characters in three novels.

Conrad, now nineteen, spent the year from February 1877 to the following February in Marseilles living extravagantly and recklessly. He attended operas and enjoyed the company of his bohemian friends in the cafes. He joined the Carlists, a political faction involved in the civil war in Spain, and for whom he and a few partners smuggled guns from the coves near Marseilles to the northeast corner of Spain. What was an adventure to Conrad ended when a Spanish patrol boat chased them, and the captain of the smuggling crew ran their boat aground near shore so that the crew could escape. During the year, Conrad had made plans for another voyage on the *Saint Antoine*, but illness prevented him from one voyage and the French military forbade him to go on the next one because Conrad had failed to obtain a permit from the Russian consul releasing him from military duty. With the three thousand francs Thaddeus had given him for the voyage, Conrad linked up with the captain of the *Mont Blanc*, who persuaded Conrad to invest in a scheme involving contraband. Conrad lost the entire three thousand francs, borrowed eight hundred francs from a friend to try to make up for the loss in the Monte Carlo casino, and lost there too. He had no money and could never again sail on a French ship. In his depression and desperation, he attempted suicide by shooting himself in the chest, but the bullet missed all important organs, and Conrad recovered in a few days.

During Conrad's years in Marseilles, his uncle Thaddeus provided him with money, advice, and emotional support. Though Thaddeus sent money when Conrad lost it, overspent, or gambled it away, it came with scoldings and advice in long letters spelling out proper attitudes and behavior. Typical in tone is one letter Conrad received after losing his trunk and family photographs:

> You have always, my dear fellow, annoyed me with your lack of order and your carefree treatment of things—in which you remind me of the Korzeniowski family—always wasting everything—and not of my dear sister, your mother, so painstaking in everything. Last year, you lost your trunk with

your things: what else was there to have in mind during a journey except yourself and your things? Now, again you have lost your family photographs and Polish books, and you want me to make up a set of one and the other! What for: So that you may again lose them at the first opportunity!! . . . So, if you don't care for cherished souvenirs (for there's no accounting for tastes, and such do exist), why clamour for them and cause others trouble? . . .

Well, there's your scolding for your lack of order in preserving your property. You really deserve a second one; for your untidy way of writing letters—I've written about this several times. Is it impossible to have a supply of paper with you and to write decently? I sincerely wish my nephew to be a decent man and that's why I scold him—though this doesn't prevent me from loving you and blessing you, my dear boy—and this I do.

Embracing you heartily, your uncle
T. Bobrowski

As one can tell from the tone of this letter, strictness did not come easily to Thaddeus. No matter how his nephew behaved, Thaddeus remained a loving and devoted uncle. In March 1878 Thaddeus received a telegram saying *"Conrad blesse, envoyez argent—arrivez"* ["Conrad wounded, send money—come"]. Thaddeus arrived in Marseilles on March 11, stayed two weeks, and paid Conrad's debts, doctor bills, and rent. But his love and generosity were not without this scolding: "You were idling for nearly a whole year—you fell into debt, you deliberately shot yourself. . . . Really, you have exceeded the limits of stupidity permitted to your age!"

The end of Conrad's stay in France marked a turning point in his life. He had learned French, his second language, and was about to leave his irresponsible, inconsiderate, passionate, depression-prone youth behind. His friend Richard Fecht helped him join a British merchant ship, and on April 24, 1878, Conrad embarked on the *Mavis*, a British freighter hauling coal to Constantinople. As a child in Poland, Conrad had vowed, "if a seaman, then an English seaman"; he had his first chance on the *Mavis*.

Conrad Becomes an English Seaman

Conrad reached England for the first time on June 18, 1878, when the *Mavis* docked at Lowestoft. He was twenty, alone and a stranger, and he spoke only a few words of English. During the next fifteen years, he would sail on seventeen ships to ports across Europe, Asia, Africa, and Australia.

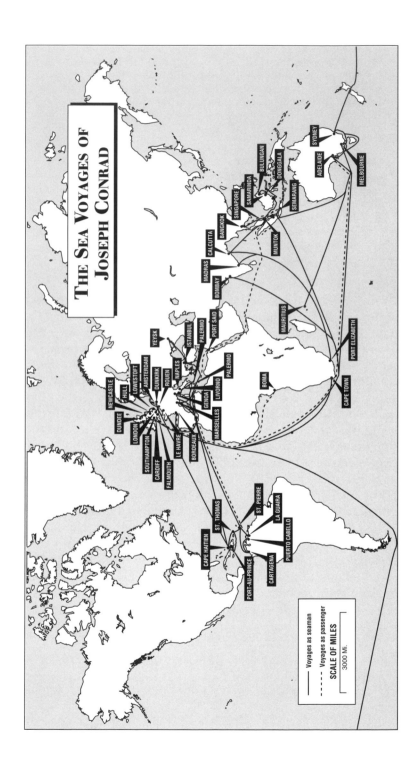

THE SEA VOYAGES OF
JOSEPH CONRAD

SYDNEY
ADELAIDE
MELBOURNE
BULUNGAN
DONGGALA
SAMARINDA
SEMARANG
SINGAPORE
BANGKOK
CALCUTTA
MADRAS
MUNTOK
BOMBAY
MAURITIUS
PORT ELIZABETH
CAPE TOWN
BOMA

YEYSK
ISTANBUL
PALERMO
PORT SAID
NAPLES
PALERMO
LIVORNO
GENOA
MARSEILLES
ROUEN
DUNKIRK
AMSTERDAM
LOWESTOFT
HULL
NEWCASTLE
DUNDEE
LONDON
SOUTHAMPTON
CARDIFF
FALMOUTH
LE HAVRE
BORDEAUX

ST. THOMAS
CAPE HAITIEN
ST. PIERRE
LA GUAIRA
PORT-AU-PRINCE
CARTAGENA
PUERTO CABELLO

Voyages as seaman
Voyages as passenger
SCALE OF MILES
3000 Mi.

Conrad worked his way from ordinary seaman to master seaman and became a naturalized British citizen during his navy career. He took and passed the exam to become second mate in June 1880. During the winter of 1884, Conrad passed the first-mate exam. Conrad became a British subject on August 19, 1886, and a month later his uncle wrote, "I am extremely glad that you have completed your naturalization, and clasp my Englishman to my breast as well as my nephew." Three months later, on November 10, Conrad passed the examination for a master's certificate, which allowed him to be the captain of a ship. This exam required knowledge of winds, currents, navigation, nautical astronomy, instruments, and measurements, much of which required mathematical calculations. His uncle wrote an ecstatic reply to his nephew's achievement: "Long live the *'Ordin: Master British Merchant Service'!* May he live as long as possible! May he be healthy and may every success meet him in every enterprise on sea and on land!" Conrad's reaction, however, was more subdued. He recalls in *A Personal Record:*

> It was a fact, I said to myself, that I was now a British master mariner beyond a doubt. It was not that I had an exaggerated sense of that very modest achievement, with which, however, luck, opportunity, or any extraneous influence could have had nothing to do. That fact, satisfactory and obscure in itself, had for me a certain ideal significance.

He felt he had now proved he could amount to something.

Though Conrad took no notes, captains and fellow seamen, events onboard ships, and impressions of places implanted themselves in his mind, later to become part of his novels. In *Joseph Conrad: The Three Lives: A Biography,* Frederick R. Karl notes the nature of a seaman's career—hard work, poor food, inconvenience, and unsanitary conditions:

> Perhaps we fail to recognize how sheerly dangerous sailoring was, how close to drowning Conrad was, and how the "romance of the sea" was intermixed with the claims of the sea, those ships and crews who went down, marginal to the last.

THE CONGO EXPERIENCE

Unable to find work on an English ship in 1889, Conrad took a job with a Belgian company to serve for three years in the Congo. Besides having a new adventure, he would fulfill his childhood vow, "When I grow up, I shall go there." Conrad sailed as a passenger to Boma at the mouth of the Congo

River and took a smaller boat to Matadi, forty miles upriver, arriving on June 13, 1890. Matadi, an important station, had one hundred and seventy European inhabitants, four factories belonging to the English, the Portuguese, the French, and the Dutch, and a project to build a railroad from Matadi to Kinshasa. Conrad, who packed ivory in cases until the next leg of his journey, began his Congo Diary when he arrived in Matadi. His first two entries resemble Marlow's attitudes. In the first entry:

> Feel considerably in doubt about the future. Think just now that my life amongst the people (white) around here cannot be very comfortable. Intend to avoid acquaintances as much as possible.

And in the next entry:

> Prominent characteristic of the social life here; people speaking ill of each other.

On June 28 Conrad and a Mr. Harou left in a caravan with thirty-one carriers on a two-hundred-mile trek to another of the company's stations at Kinshasa. They traveled through rough, open, hilly country, through dry grass and areas of red soil, and across numerous streams and rivers. Conrad made many entries about the difficulty of open camping, poor food and water, and sleepless nights bothered by heat and mosquitoes. The travelers occasionally passed a village market, heard distant beating drums, and saw many dead corpses. On July 29, Conrad wrote: "On the road today [*sic*] passed a skeleton tied up to a post. Also white man's grave—no name—heap of stones in the form of a cross." Conrad had four fevers on this thirty-six-day trip; his companion Harou, a heavy man, was more often sick and had to be carried in a hammock, a task that made the carriers cranky.

In Kinshasa Conrad was scheduled to take command of a steamer, the *Florida*, to travel farther up the Congo River, but because it had been badly damaged, plans changed. Conrad was assigned as an assistant on the steamer, the *Roi des Belges*, to learn the river and to go to Stanley Falls to find and return the company's agent Georges Antoine Klein, who was very ill. During the voyage the captain became ill, and Conrad was put temporarily in command. Though Conrad made the trip in particularly good time, Klein nevertheless died on the way back. This voyage forms the basis for *Heart of Darkness*, and Klein corresponds to Kurtz although no information exists to indicate whether their characters are

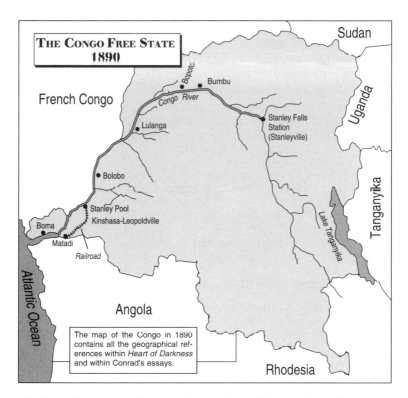

THE CONGO FREE STATE
1890

Sudan

French Congo

Bopoto

Bumbu

Congo River

Lulanga

Stanley Falls
Station
(Stanleyville)

Uganda

Bolobo

Stanley Pool
Kinshasa-Leopoldville

Boma

Matadi

Railroad

Atlantic Ocean

Angola

Tanganyika

Lake Tanganyika

The map of the Congo in 1890
contains all the geographical references within *Heart of Darkness*
and within Conrad's essays.

Rhodesia

similar. Conrad said that in writing *Heart of Darkness* he
"pushed a little (only a little) beyond the actual facts of the
case."

On his return to Kinshasa, Conrad, who had had a five-
day bout with dysentery in Stanley Falls, was in poor health,
and he could not get the command of a steamer as planned.
Consequently, he decided to return to England and travel
downriver to Boma. In *A Personal Record*, Conrad recalls: "I
arrived at that delectable capital Boma, where before the departure of the steamer which was to take me home I had the
time to wish myself dead over and over again with perfect
sincerity." Conrad's Congo illness undermined his health
permanently, making him susceptible to fevers and gouty
symptoms (pain in the joints) for the rest of his life. Conrad
returned to England in January 1891 and entered a London
hospital to try to recover. He was sick, out of work, and depressed.

Thirty years after his Congo experience, Conrad was still
indignant at the greed of Europeans who took part in what

he called in *Last Essays* "the vilest scramble for loot that ever disfigured the history of human conscience and geographical exploration." In *Heart of Darkness* Marlow's criticism of the Roman settlers in Britain is merely a disguise for Conrad's opinion of the colonizers:

> They were no colonists; their administration was merely a squeeze and nothing more, I suspect. They were conquerors, and for that you want only brute force—nothing to boast of, when you have it, since your strength is just an accident arising from the weakness of others. They grabbed what they could get for the sake of what was to be got. It was just robbery with violence, aggravated murder on a great scale, and men going at it blind—as is very proper for those who tackle a darkness. The conquest of the earth, which mostly means the taking it away from those who have a different complexion or slightly flatter noses than ourselves, is not a pretty thing when you look into it too much.

CONRAD BEGINS TO WRITE

For a short time Conrad's sea career, which was losing its appeal, overlapped his writing, which increasingly interested him. He had written his first story, "The Black Mate," in 1886 for a competition sponsored by a magazine. He wrote nothing more until 1889 when he started *Almayer's Folly,* which, he claims in *A Personal Record,* began without intention:

> I never made a note of a fact, of an impression or of an anecdote in my life. The conception of a planned book was entirely outside my mental range when I sat down to write; the ambition of being an author had never turned up amongst these gracious imaginary existences one creates fondly for oneself at times in the stillness and immobility of a day-dream.

Conrad worked on *Almayer's Folly* for three years. In July 1894 he sent the completed manuscript under the pseudonym Kamudi to the publisher Fisher Unwin, who bought it for £20 and published it. All reviews were encouraging, especially noting Conrad's adventurous use of language; H.G. Wells wrote in the *Saturday Review* that it was "exceedingly well imagined and well written, and it will certainly secure Mr. Conrad a high place among contemporary story tellers."

In October that year Conrad met Edward Garnett, a reader for Unwin, who encouraged Conrad to write another novel. Conrad, who began *An Outcast of the Islands* the evening after his conversation with Garnett, set it in the same area of the Pacific Islands as *Almayer's Folly,* used many of the same characters, and addressed themes of betrayal and retribution. Published in 1896, *An Outcast* got many good reviews; H.G. Wells, writing in the *Saturday Review*, criticized Conrad's wordiness but thought it the best book published in that year. Of Conrad he said, "He writes so as to mask and dishonor the greatness in him. Greatness is deliberately written. . . . Only greatness could make books of which the detailed workmanship was so copiously bad, so well worth reading, so convincing, and so stimulating."

Conrad was often asked why he wrote in English rather than in his native Polish or in French. Jokingly he explained that "I value our beautiful [Polish] literature too highly to introduce into it my inept fumbling." By the time Conrad wrote his first novel, he had been speaking English for eleven years. Conrad had learned conversational English from the fishermen and sailors in a little inn in Lowestoft where he stayed between voyages. Analyses of the sentences in the newspaper *Standard*, the only literature in the seaport town, were his first lessons in English. Conrad learned literary English by studying Shakespeare's plays and Lord Byron's poems aboard ship. He explained to his friend Hugh Walpole in 1918:

> When I wrote the first words of *Almayer's Folly*, I had been already for years and years *thinking* in English. I began to think in English long before I mastered, I won't say the style (I haven't done that yet), but the mere uttered speech. . . . You may take it from me that if I had not known English I wouldn't have written a line for print, in my life.

CONRAD BEGINS A NEW LIFE ON LAND

In November 1894 Conrad met Jessie George, who was twenty-one and pretty. She was not Conrad's intellectual equal, but her disposition complemented Conrad's; her emotional steadiness offset Conrad's moods. From a large working-class family, she had little formal education, but she had worked as a typist and often typed Conrad's manuscripts. Her memoirs describe pleasant times during their year-long courtship that ended when Conrad proposed rather abruptly early in 1896: "Look here, my dear, we had better get married and out of this. Look at the weather. We will get married at once and get over to France. How soon can you be ready? In a week—a fortnight?" His urgency arose not from his passion for her but from his concern about his health and his work and his notion that he would not live long. They were married on March 24, 1896, at the St. George Register Office in London and went immediately to an island off the coast of Brittany in France where Conrad set to work on *The Rescuers*. When the couple returned, they lived at Ivy Walls, Stanford-le-Hope, Essex, in western England. The Conrads had two sons, Borys, born January 15, 1898, and John Alexander, born August 2, 1906.

Besides his devoted wife, Conrad gathered around him a group of loyal and helpful friends. One of his first English friends, G.F.W. Hope, introduced him to Jessie and remained a friend for life; another, Adolf Krieger, often lent Conrad money. Ford Madox Ford, whom Conrad met in 1898, collaborated with Conrad on stories and helped him reconstruct a story that burned accidentally in a fire at his desk. Edward Garnett encouraged Conrad when he doubted his ability to write and published favorable essays on Conrad's work. In one of his most chaotic periods, Conrad found J.B. Pinker, who served as Conrad's agent. He drew up budgets to get Conrad's debts under control and maintained his equanimity when Conrad did not abide by them. Conrad particularly liked John Galsworthy and helped him with his first novel, *Jocelyn*. Galsworthy lent Conrad money and paid his doctor bills and insurance premiums. Conrad often wrote to one or another of these friends when he was sick, broke, depressed, or unable to find his way in a story, and his friends came to his rescue. Collectively, they played a role similar to that of Thaddeus in Conrad's youth.

CONRAD'S EARLY GREAT WORKS

Between 1897 and 1904, Conrad published nine of his most significant works. *The Nigger of the 'Narcissus,'* published in 1897, was a turning point in Conrad's career and his imagination. Frederick Karl explains that he shifted "his concern from Malay subjects to a much deeper and more intense concern with life and death, the mythical sea and the transient individual, survival itself, themes which in ensuing years would become his major subject matter." His next volume, a collection of short stories, *Tales of Unrest,* published in 1898, includes "The Idiots," "Karain," "An Outpost of Progress," "The Return," and "The Lagoon." As was his usual practice, Conrad was working on several stories at the same time. In a letter to Cunninghame Graham, Conrad confided that his writing of *Lord Jim* was detained because he was struggling with his philosophy: He saw "no morality, no knowledge and no hope; there is only the consciousness of ourselves which drives us about a world that whether seen in a concave or convex mirror is always a vain and floating experience." Graham responded and Conrad found his way out of his dilemma by creating the narrator Marlow to introduce order. Marlow first appeared in "Youth," a story based on Conrad's experiences on the *Palestine.* With Marlow as narrator, Conrad was able to continue writing *Lord Jim,* and find a balance for his theme, dream versus realism. *Lord Jim,* published in 1900, drew rave reviews; typical was one appearing in the *Manchester Guardian:*

> Mr. Joseph Conrad's work has long been known to novel readers who search for their literature, and to them the publication of *Lord Jim* may rank as a memorable event. It is not to be accepted easily, it cannot be read in a half dose, and by the great public which multiplies editions it may remain neglected or unknown. Yet it is of such remarkable originality and merit that one may look for an emphasis of critical opinion which . . . can force a great reputation in the face of popular apathy or distaste.

During this flurry of writing, Conrad found time to collaborate with Ford Madox Ford on two stories they hoped would reach a wide audience, *The Inheritors,* published in 1901, and *Romance,* published in 1903.

Conrad's next work, *Typhoon,* was published in 1902. The main character, McWhirr, was based on the captain of the *Highland Forest. Typhoon* explores a theme similar to that of *Lord Jim,* imagination versus pragmatism, only in reverse: Jim has too much imagination, McWhirr too little. *Typhoon* also elicited high praise. It was republished in 1903 as part of a collection, *Typhoon and Other Stories,* which included "Amy Foster," "Tomorrow," and "Falk." After the short stories, Conrad again used the narrator Marlow in *Heart of Darkness.* The slow trip by river through the dense tropical jungle symbolizes Conrad's complex exploration of evil in the heart of the Congo. First serialized in 1899, it was published in a collection, *Youth: A Narrative, and Two Other Stories,* in 1902 along with "The End of the Tether," a story based on Conrad's time in Singapore and voyages to Borneo on the *Vidar.*

Conrad worked from December 1902 until August 1904 on his longest, most complex novel, *Nostromo.* Baines describes it as "Conrad's most ambitious feat of imagination. . . . He chose a far larger canvas than he had used before or was to use again; it is as large as that of any great novel except *War and Peace." Nostromo* takes place in Costaguana, a fictional country Conrad created from readings and from the brief stops he made in South America and the Caribbean while sailing on the *Saint Antoine* in 1876. Its theme is colonialism; according to Jeffrey Meyers in *Joseph Conrad: A Biography*, it addresses three implied questions: "What is the meaning of civilization and progress? What happens when materialism replaces human values? How does colonialism affect traditional societies?" This time the reviews were not good, however, and Conrad was disappointed. One critic said the story was too hard to follow and contained too many digressions and irrelevant details, but it "will repay those who give it the close attention it deserves." Reviewers recognized in Conrad's works a new kind of writing. Karl explains that the difference "was, of course, connected to Conrad's modernity. 'I am Modern,' he had trumpeted, himself, and that movement away from the Zolaesque social unit toward the less directly ethical, the less explicit, the more purely aesthetic was a measure of this novelty." In short, Conrad's novels focus not on plot and character, nor on social criticism, but on artistic style and inner truth.

TROUBLES AND MISHAPS IN CONRAD'S PERSONAL LIFE

After finishing *Nostromo,* Conrad needed a change and a rest. But first he took Jessie to London in October 1904 for a knee operation to repair damage from an 1889 skating accident that had left her partially crippled, the first of a dozen unsuccessful operations. For thirty years Jessie had trouble walking, and she compensated for her handicap by sitting, eating sweets, reading "trashy" novels, playing dominoes, and gaining weight until obesity made mobility even harder.

Three months after the surgery, the Conrads set off for a vacation on the island of Capri in the Mediterranean, but the trip was anything but relaxing. Conrad had mislaid his favorite eyeglasses and had to leave without them. Jessie forgot part of her false teeth. Since she could barely walk, Jessie had to be carried in chairs. Boarding the ship in Dover, one carrier got his hand stuck between the chair and the gangrail; horrified onlookers feared she would be tipped into the water. In Rome her chair slipped out of a railway carriage, and she was left hanging onto a door. At Naples the sea was too rough for Jessie to travel, so they were held up there for five days. Jessie's nurse got sick, and Conrad caught influenza and bronchitis and could not sleep because of jangled nerves. He wrote to Galsworthy in January:

> The delay of all these days in the hotel has utterly ruined me. . . . The nervous irritation of these days in Naples has prevented me from doing anything. . . . But the whole expedition is a mad thing really, for it rests upon what I am not certain of—my power to produce some sixty thousand words in four months. I feel sick with apprehension at times.

And to Pinker in February:

> I, who now if ever wanted peace to concentrate my thoughts after all the anxieties in London, could not achieve it (as you may guess) in these lodgings. I have worked but badly—there's no use disguising the truth—I've been in a state of exasperation with the eternal something cropping up to distract my mind.

When Conrad was nearly out of the money his friends had provided him for the trip and Pinker had advanced him all that he could, Conrad received news that, by the king's consent, he had been awarded a grant of £500. Relieved, the Conrads went back to England in May.

The trip to Capri characterizes the kind of money troubles, mishaps, and illnesses that plagued the family until near the end of Conrad's life. Conrad spent beyond his income and consistently negotiated for advances on writing he promised to do, a situation that put great strain on his nerves and health and brought on fevers and symptoms of gout. He insisted that he had to get away periodically to relieve the tension of writing, but every trip was a disaster. On a trip to Montpellier, France, Borys got sick, Conrad's pocket money was stolen, and he started a mattress fire from a lighted cigarette. On a trip to Poland just before World War I, he and Jessie had to hide in a country house to prevent being taken into custody as British citizens until the ambassador could arrange an escape route through Italy. In 1905 Jessie had a nervous breakdown, Borys had scarlet fever, and two months later his skin was burned when the nurse put too much disinfectant in his bathwater. Karl offers an explanation for the chaotic pattern of Conrad's life:

> This accumulation of anxieties, worries, fears, and assorted guilt feelings was connected, evidently, to his way of working and to the functioning of his literary imagination. Apparently, he could not work effectively unless he were close to breakdown, on the edge of psychic disorders, ill in body and mind. Conrad's physical disorders were legion: recurring gout (a hereditary condition), arthritis, delirious fevers, neuralgia, influenza. These, however, were simply the tip. The inner disorder was far greater, and when it was at its most intense, he functioned most effectively artistically.

CONRAD'S LATER WORKS

For fifteen years after the publication of *Nostromo* in 1904, Conrad's life continued much as it had since his marriage. He was sick, he had money problems, he moved to Kent in south-eastern England, he enjoyed his old friends and made a few new ones, and he wrote voluminously. Conrad was forty-seven years old in 1904; still to come were eight novels and part of a ninth, six collections of stories and essays, two autobiographical pieces, an essay on politics, and three plays. *The Mirror of the Sea* (1906) is a collection of essays describing episodes from his sailing days. *The Secret Agent* (1907), which had mediocre sales, is a psychological-political detective novel that was adapted as a play. Conrad struggled with *Under Western Eyes* (1911) for more than two years; set in Russia and Switzerland, it tells the story of Razumov, who commits a crime in the first part and confesses and tries to redeem himself in the second. After completing the manuscript in 1910, Conrad suffered a nervous breakdown which required rest and attentive care from Jessie. After his recovery, he wrote *Some Reminiscences*, also called *A Personal Record* (1912), and a collection of stories, *Twixt Land and Sea* (1912), which includes the famous story "The Secret Sharer." *Victory* (1915), also adapted as a play, is a story set in the Malay Archipelago about the theme of isolation. Jeffrey Meyers calls *The Shadow-Line* (1917) Conrad's last great work; it is a story based on Conrad's experiences on the *Ortago* sailing from Bangkok to Singapore in 1888. Meyers explains that

> the title of the story refers not only to that twilight region between the naive self-confidence of youth and the more introspective wisdom of maturity, but also to the entrance to the Gulf of Siam, where the former captain was buried and where the ship is mysteriously becalmed off the island of Koh-ring (which also appeared in "The Secret Sharer").

THE WAR YEARS

During World War I, Conrad, now in his late fifties, volunteered as an observer to write promotional pieces on Allied plane and ship activities. His first assignment was an air flight from the Lowestoft Royal Naval Station. In November 1916 he sailed from Granton, near Edinburgh, to repair nets that defended the port from German submarines. He was aboard a twelve-day cruise on the HMS *Ready*, flying under a Norwegian flag and disguised as a merchant ship to entice German subs into a trap. Conrad was exhilarated to be at sea again; his son John said that his father "changed from the gouty invalid I knew to an able and energetic seaman almost as soon as his feet touched the deck." Conrad wrote "Flight," "Well Done!" "Tradition," and "The Unlighted Coast" as a result of these experiences. The war was bad for Conrad's son, however. After Borys failed the exams for entrance to the university, he was commissioned to the Mechanical Transport Corps in 1915, the beginning of a military career. Fighting on the French front a month before Armistice Day, he was gassed and shell-shocked, but recovered after hospitalization. Conrad's worry for his son was coupled with joy when the end of the war brought freedom and independence to his native Poland after 123 years of foreign oppression.

SUCCESS AND FAME

The immediate postwar period brought Conrad financial security and fame. Conrad's popularity really began when Alfred Knopf of Doubleday Publishers in America launched an advertising campaign for *Chance,* marketing it with an attractive cover jacket and catchy chapter titles. The novel sold ten thousand copies. Popularity continued to grow with the publications of *Victory* and *The Shadow-Line. Under Western Eyes* sold four thousand copies, *The Rover* twenty-six thousand. Between 1914 and 1923 six volumes were published about Conrad: three of criticism, a bibliography, and two memoirs. In 1919 the play adaptation of *Victory* had a successful three-month theatrical run at the Globe in London. Doubleday published a collected edition of Conrad's works.

Conrad's income grew with growing popularity and increased sales, enough to free him of debt and provide him with money to match his spending habits. Besides a regular two thousand pounds a year, he received a twelve-thousand-dollar advance on the American collected edition in 1921 and ten thousand pounds on the deluxe English collected edition in 1922. The sale of serial rights for *The Rescue* and film rights for *Victory* earned him another six thousand pounds.

In 1923 Doubleday invited Conrad to America for readings from his works, but fearing his English had too strong a Polish accent, Conrad first practiced on home audiences. Doubleday tried to arrange a quiet entrance into New York Harbor, but pandemonium broke out when Conrad arrived. He wrote to Jessie: "I will not attempt to describe to you my landing because it is indescribable. To be aimed at by forty cameras held by forty men [that looked as if they came out of the slums] is a nerve-shattering experience." Conrad gave a lecture and reading from *Victory* to an audience of two hundred invited guests at the home of railroad magnate Arthur Curtiss James. In his nervousness, Conrad slipped into a heavy Polish accent, but the audience applauded his performance. Of his American trip, he told a friend: "I felt all the time like a man *dans un avion* [in an airplane], in a mist, in a cloud, in a vapour of idealistic phraseology; I was lost, bewildered, amused—but frightened as well."

In addition to his popularity and financial success, Conrad won recognition from the academic community, the prime minister, and fellow artists. He was offered honorary degrees from the universities of Oxford, Cambridge, Edinburgh, Liverpool, and Durham, but declined all, claiming a desire to stay out of the university tradition since he had not finished high school nor attended any university. In May 1924 Prime Minister Ramsey MacDonald sent him an offer of knighthood (Conrad thought the envelope contained his tax bill), but he refused this honor, too. He dreamed of a Nobel Prize, but was never nominated. Painters and sculptors who sought Conrad as a subject have left twenty-six paintings and sketches of him. The most famous artist, Jacob Epstein, sculpted a bust of Conrad. By this time Conrad was too sickly to enjoy his fame. On July 3, 1924, he told a friend: "I feel (and probably look) horribly limp and my spirits stand at about zero. Here you have the horrid truth. But I haven't been well for a long time and *strictly entre nous* [strictly between us] I begin to feel like a cornered rat."

Conrad's death came in August 1924. Friends and his sons had gathered at his home for a holiday weekend on August 1. While taking a friend for a drive, Conrad suffered a mild heart attack and turned back. Doctors came on Saturday and pronounced his condition normal, but Conrad was weak and his breathing heavy. Early on Sunday morning on August 3, Conrad insisted on sitting up in a chair; two hours later he was found dead on the floor. Jessie arranged a Catholic funeral mass on August 7 at St. Thomas Catholic Church in Canterbury. Ironically, his funeral took place at the same time as the Canterbury Cricket Festival, and the town was decorated with banners and filled with tourists. Though Jessie's old leg infirmity prevented her from attending, Conrad's sons and loyal old and new friends gathered at the service, described by Meyers.

At the graveside in Canterbury cemetery Father Shepherd read the Catholic burial service. "So we left him," Graham wrote, "with his sails all duly furled, ropes flemished down, and with the anchor holding truly in the kind Kentish earth." The moving epigraph from Spenser's *The Faerie Queene*, which Conrad had used on the title page of *The Rover*, was cut into the grey granite:

Sleep after toyle, port after stormie seas,
Ease after warre, death after life, does greatly please.

CHAPTER 1

Major Themes in *Heart of Darkness*

READINGS ON
HEART OF DARKNESS

A Mythical Journey into the Self

Albert J. Guerard

Albert J. Guerard concedes that *Heart of Darkness* can be read as autobiography, travelogue, and political criticism, but it is more significantly read as a symbolic journey into the self, a journey through the human dark side. In his elaboration of this theme, Guerard identifies the methods and techniques Conrad uses to create the dreamlike qualities that make the novel powerful. Albert J. Guerard taught English at Stanford University in California. He is the author of six novels and critical works on Thomas Hardy, André Gide, Charles Dickens, Fyodor Dostoyevsky, and William Faulkner.

Historically speaking, [Conrad's short works, *Heart of Darkness*, "The Secret Sharer", and *The Shadow Line*] are among the first and best—one is tempted to say only—symbolist masterpieces in English fiction. The sea voyages and the one great Congo journey are unmistakably journeys within, and journeys through a darkness.

The matter may come to seem dark indeed, so a brief forewarning is necessary. The term and concept of the *night journey*, borrowed from anthropology and now gaining some currency in criticism, will appear several times in the following pages. By it I refer to the archetypal myth dramatized in much great literature since the Book of Jonah: the story of an essentially solitary journey involving profound spiritual change in the voyager. In its classical form the journey is a descent into the earth, followed by a return to light. Sometimes the dream is literally an illuminating dream (as with Don Quixote's experience in the well); more often it is dramatized through an actual voyage and movement through space. A familiar variant concerns passage through

Adapted from excerpts of *Conrad the Novelist*, by Albert J. Guerard (Cambridge, MA: Harvard University Press, 1958) by permission of the author.

a tunnel or other dark place; another describes descent to the depths of the sea. It is assumed that this myth, like any powerful and universal dream, has some other meaning than one of literal adventure, though this other meaning is often unintended. *We dream this dream because we are the people we are; because our conscious and unconscious lives alike have certain psychic needs.* The nature of the vision may vary; so too may vary the nature of the change and rebirth experienced.

But very often the dream appears to be about the introspective process itself: about a risky descent into the preconscious or even unconscious; about a restorative return to the primitive sources of being and an advance through temporary regression. . . .

AUTOBIOGRAPHY, TRAVELOGUE, AND POLITICAL CRITICISM

"Heart of Darkness" is the most famous of these personal short novels: a *Pilgrim's Progress* for our pessimistic and psychologizing age. "Before the Congo I was just a mere animal."[1] . . . The autobiographical basis of the narrative is well known, and its introspective bias obvious; this is Conrad's longest journey into self. But it is well to remember that "Heart of Darkness" is also other if more superficial things: a sensitive and vivid travelogue, and a comment on "the vilest scramble for loot that ever disfigured the history of human conscience and geographical exploration."[2] The Congo was much in the public mind in 1889. . . .

"Heart of Darkness" has its important public side, as an angry document on absurd and brutal exploitation. Marlow is treated to the spectacle of a French man-of-war shelling an unseen "enemy" village in the bush, and presently he will wander into the grove at the first company station where the starving and sick Negroes withdraw to die. It is one of the greatest of Conrad's many moments of compassionate rendering. The compassion extends even to the cannibal crew of the [Congo steamer] *Roi des Belges*. Deprived of the rotten hippo meat they had brought along for food, and paid three nine-inch pieces of brass wire a week, they appear to subsist on "lumps of some stuff like half-cooked dough, of a dirty lavender color" which they keep wrapped in leaves. Conrad

1. Conrad reportedly made this comment to his friend and critic Edward Garnett. 2. from Conrad's *Last Essays*

here operates through ambiguous suggestion (are the lumps human flesh?) but elsewhere he wants, like Gide after him, to make his complacent European reader *see:* see, for instance, the drunken unkempt official met on the road and three miles farther on the body of the Negro with a bullet hole in his forehead. "Heart of Darkness" is a record of things seen and done. But also Conrad was reacting to the humanitarian pretenses of some of the looters precisely as the novelist today reacts to the moralisms of cold-war propaganda. Then it was ivory that poured from the heart of darkness; now it is uranium. Conrad shrewdly recognized— an intuition amply developed in *Nostromo*—that deception is most sinister when it becomes self-deception, and the propagandist takes seriously his own fictions. Kurtz "could get himself to believe anything—anything." The benevolent rhetoric of his seventeen-page report for the International Society for the Suppression of Savage Customs was meant sincerely enough. But a deeper sincerity spoke through his scrawled postscript: "Exterminate all the brutes!" The conservative Conrad . . . speaks through the journalist who says that "Kurtz's proper sphere ought to have been politics 'on the popular side.'"

Conrad, again like many novelists today, was both drawn to idealism and repelled by its hypocritical abuse. "The conquest of the earth, which mostly means the taking it away from those who have a different complexion or slightly flatter noses than ourselves, is not a pretty thing when you look into it too much. What redeems it is the idea only. An idea at the back of it; not a sentimental pretence but an idea; and an unselfish belief in the idea." Marlow commits himself to the yet unseen agent partly because Kurtz "had come out equipped with moral ideas of some sort." Anything would seem preferable to the demoralized greed and total cynicism of the others, "the flabby devil" of the Central Station. Later, when he discovers what has happened to Kurtz's moral ideas, he remains faithful to the "nightmare of my choice." In *Under Western Eyes* Sophia Antonovna makes a distinction between those who burn and those who rot, and remarks that it is sometimes preferable to burn. The Kurtz who had made himself literally one of the devils of the land, and who in solitude had kicked himself loose of the earth, burns while the others rot. Through violent not flabby evil he exists in the moral universe even before pronouncing judgment on himself with his dying breath. A little too much has been made, I think, of the redemptive value of those two words—"The horror!" But none of the company "pilgrims" could have uttered them.

THE VALUE OF SOCIETAL RESTRAINTS AND THE WORK ETHIC

The redemptive view is Catholic, of course, though no priest was in attendance; Kurtz can repent as the gunman of [Graham Greene's] *The Power and the Glory* cannot. "Heart of Darkness" (still at this public and wholly conscious level) combines a Victorian ethic and late Victorian fear of the white man's deterioration with a distinctly Catholic psychology. We are protected from ourselves by society with its laws and its watchful neighbors, Marlow observes. And we are protected by work. "You wonder I didn't go ashore for a howl and a dance? Well, no—I didn't. Fine sentiments, you say? Fine sentiments, be hanged! I had no time. I had to mess about with white-lead and strips of woolen blanket helping to put bandages on those leaky steam-pipes." But when the external restraints of society and work are removed, we must meet the challenge and temptation of savage reversion with our "own inborn strength. Principles won't do." This inborn strength appears to include restraint —the restraint that Kurtz lacked and the cannibal crew of the *Roi des Belges* surprisingly possessed. The hollow man, whose evil is the evil of *vacancy*, succumbs. And in their different degrees the pilgrims and Kurtz share this hollowness. "Perhaps there was nothing within" the manager of the Central Station. "Such a suspicion made one pause—for out there there were no external checks." And there was nothing inside the brickmaker, that papier-maché Mephistopheles,[3] "but a little loose dirt, maybe."

As for Kurtz, the wilderness "echoed loudly within him because he was hollow at the core." Perhaps the chief contradiction of "Heart of Darkness" is that it suggests and dramatizes evil as an active energy (Kurtz and his unspeakable lusts) but defines evil as vacancy. The primitive (and here the contradiction is only verbal) is compact of passion and apathy. "I was struck by the fire of his eyes and the composed languor of his expression. . . . This shadow looked satiated and calm, as though for the moment it had had its fill

3. the evil spirit to whom the legendary Faust sold his soul

of all the emotions." Of the two menaces—the unspeakable desires and the apathy—apathy surely seemed the greater to Conrad. Hence we cannot quite believe the response of Marlow's heart to the beating of the tom-toms. This is, I think, the story's minor but central flaw, and the source of an unfruitful ambiguity: that it slightly overdoes the kinship with the "passionate uproar," slightly undervalues the temptation of inertia.

In any event, it is time to recognize that the story is not primarily about Kurtz or about the brutality of Belgian officials but about Marlow its narrator. To what extent it also expresses the Joseph Conrad a biographer might conceivably recover, who in 1898 still felt a debt must be paid for his Congo journey and who paid it by the writing of this story, is doubtless an insoluble question. I suspect two facts (of a possible several hundred) are important. First, that going to the Congo was the enactment of a childhood wish associated with the disapproved childhood ambition to go to sea, and that this belated enactment was itself profoundly disapproved, in 1890, by the uncle and guardian. It was another gesture of a man bent on throwing his life away. But even more important may be the guilt of complicity, just such a guilt as many novelists of the Second World War have been obliged to work off. What Conrad thought of the expedition of the Katanga Company of 1890–1892 is accurately reflected in his remarks on the "Eldorado Exploring Expedition" of "Heart of Darkness": "It was reckless without hardihood, greedy without audacity, and cruel without courage . . . with no more moral purpose at the back of it than there is in burglars breaking into a safe." Yet Conrad hoped to obtain command of the expedition's ship even after he had returned from the initiatory voyage dramatized in his novel. Thus the adventurous Conrad and Conrad the moralist may have experienced collision. But the collision, again as with so many novelists of the second war, could well have been deferred and retrospective, not felt intensely at the time.

MARLOW'S SPIRITUAL VOYAGE OF SELF-DISCOVERY

So much for the elusive Conrad of the biographers and of the "Congo Diary." Substantially and in its central emphasis "Heart of Darkness" concerns Marlow (projection to whatever great or small degree of a more irrecoverable Conrad) and his journey toward and through certain facets or potentialities of self. [Critic] F.R. Leavis seems to regard him as a narrator only, providing a "specific and concretely realized point of view." But Marlow reiterates often enough that he is recounting a spiritual voyage of self-discovery. He remarks casually but crucially that he did not know himself before setting out, and that he likes work for the chance it provides to "find yourself . . . what no other man can ever know." The Inner Station "was the farthest point of navigation and the culminating point of my experience." At a material and rather superficial level, the journey is through the temptation of atavism.[4] It is a record of "remote kinship" with the "wild and passionate uproar," of a "trace of a response" to it, of a final rejection of the "fascination of the abomination." And why should there not be the trace of a response? "The mind of man is capable of anything—because everything is in it, all the past as well as all the future." Marlow's temptation is made concrete through his exposure to Kurtz, a white man and sometime idealist who had fully responded to the wilderness: a potential and fallen self. "I had turned to the wilderness really, not to Mr. Kurtz." At the climax Marlow follows Kurtz ashore, confounds the beat of the drum with the beating of his heart, goes through the ordeal of looking into Kurtz's "mad soul," and brings him back to the ship. He returns to Europe a changed and more knowing man. Ordinary people are now "intruders whose knowledge of life was to me an irritating pretence, because I felt so sure they could not possibly know the things I knew."

On this literal plane, and when the events are so abstracted from the dream-sensation conveying them, it is hard to take Marlow's plight very seriously. Will he, the busy captain and moralizing narrator, also revert to savagery, go ashore for a howl and a dance, indulge unspeakable lusts? . . .

THE NIGHT JOURNEY AND ITS DREAMLIKE QUALITY

The personal narrative is unmistakably authentic, which means that it explores something truer, more fundamental, and distinctly less material: the night journey into the unconscious, and confrontation of an entity within the self. "I flung one shoe overboard, and became aware that that was exactly what I had been looking forward to—a talk with

4. a throwback; a reversion to an ancestral form and manner

Kurtz." It little matters what, in terms of psychological symbolism, we call this double or say he represents: whether the Freudian id or the Jungian shadow or more vaguely the outlaw. And I am afraid it is impossible to say where Conrad's conscious understanding of his story began and ended. The important thing is that the introspective plunge and powerful dream seem true; and are therefore inevitably moving.

Certain circumstances of Marlow's voyage, looked at in these terms, take on a new importance. The true night journey can occur (except during analysis) only in sleep or in the waking dream of a profoundly intuitive mind. Marlow insists more than is necessary on the dreamlike quality of his narrative. "It seems to me I am trying to tell you a dream —making a vain attempt, because no relation of a dream can convey the dream-sensation, that commingling of absurdity, surprise, and bewilderment in a tremor of struggling revolt . . ." Even before leaving Brussels Marlow felt as though he "were about to set off for the center of the earth," not the center of a continent. The introspective voyager leaves his familiar rational world, is "cut off from the comprehension" of his surroundings; his steamer toils "along slowly on the edge of a black and incomprehensible frenzy." As the crisis approaches, the dreamer and his ship move through a silence that "seemed unnatural, like a state of trance"; then enter (a few miles below the Inner Station) a deep fog. "The approach to this Kurtz grubbing for ivory in the wretched bush was beset by as many dangers as though he had been an enchanted princess sleeping in a fabulous castle." Later, Marlow's task is to try "to break the spell" of the wilderness that holds Kurtz entranced.

The approach to the unconscious and primitive may be aided by a savage or half-savage guide, and may require the token removal of civilized trappings or aids. . . . In "Heart of Darkness" the token "relinquishment" and the death of the half-savage guide are connected. The helmsman falling at Marlow's feet casts blood on his shoes, which he is "morbidly anxious" to change and in fact throws overboard. . . . Here we have presumably entered an area of unconscious creation; the dream is true but the teller may have no idea why it is. So too, possibly, a psychic need as well as literary tact compelled Conrad to defer the meeting between Marlow and Kurtz for some three thousand words after announcing that it took place. We think we are about to meet Kurtz at last. But instead Marlow leaps ahead to his meeting with the "Intended"; comments on Kurtz's megalomania and assumption of his place among the devils of the land; reports on the seventeen-page pamphlet; relates his meeting and conversation with Kurtz's harlequin disciple—and only then tells of seeing through his binoculars the heads on the stakes surrounding Kurtz's house. This is the "evasive" Conrad in full play, deferring what we most want to know and see; perhaps compelled to defer climax in this way. The tactic is dramatically effective, though possibly carried to excess: we are told on the authority of completed knowledge certain things we would have found hard to believe had they been presented through a slow consecutive realistic discovery. But also it can be argued that it was psychologically impossible for Marlow to go at once to Kurtz's house with the others. The double must be brought on board the ship, and the first confrontation must occur there. . . .

MARLOW CONFRONTS KURTZ AND THE DARKNESS

Hence the shock Marlow experiences when he discovers that Kurtz's cabin is empty and his secret sharer gone; a part of himself has vanished. "What made this emotion so overpowering was—how shall I define it?—the moral shock I received, as if something altogether monstrous, intolerable to thought and odious to the soul, had been thrust upon me unexpectedly." And now he must risk the ultimate confrontation in a true solitude and must do so on shore. "I was anxious to deal with this shadow by myself alone—and to this day I don't know why I was so jealous of sharing with anyone the peculiar blackness of that experience." He follows the crawling Kurtz through the grass; comes upon him "long, pale, indistinct, like a vapor exhaled by the earth." ("I had cut him off cleverly . . .") We are told very little of what Kurtz said in the moments that follow; and little of his incoherent discourses after he is brought back to the ship. "His was an impenetrable darkness. I looked at him as you peer down at a man who is lying at the bottom of a precipice where the sun never shines"—a comment less vague and rhetorical, in terms of psychic geography, than it may seem at a first reading. And then Kurtz is dead, taken off the ship, his body buried in a "muddy hole." With the confrontation over, Marlow must still emerge from environing darkness, and does so through that other deep fog of sickness. The identification is not yet completely broken. "And it is not my own extremity I remember best—a vision of grayness without form filled with physical pain, and a careless contempt for the evanescence of all things—even of this pain itself. No! It is his extremity that I seem to have lived through." Only in the atonement of his lie to Kurtz's "Intended," back in the sepulchral city, does the experience come truly to an end. "I laid the ghost of his gifts at last with a lie . . ." Such seems to be the content of the dream. . . .

CONRAD'S METHOD IS UNSPOKEN, SHADOWY, AND IMPRESSIONISTIC

I am willing to grant that the unspeakable rites and unspeakable secrets become wearisome, but the fact—at once literary and psychological—is that they must remain *unspoken*. A confrontation with such a double and facet of the unconscious cannot be reported through realistic dialogue; the conversations must remain as shadowy as the narrator's conversations with Leggatt[5]. So too when Marlow finds it hard to define the moral shock he received on seeing the empty cabin, or when he says he doesn't know why he was jealous of sharing his experience, I think we can take him literally . . . and in a sense even be thankful for his uncertainty. . . .

"I listened on the watch for the sentence, for the word, that would give me the clue to the faint uneasiness inspired by this narrative that seemed to shape itself without human lips in the heavy night air of the river." Thus one of Marlow's listeners, the original "I" who frames the story, comments on its initial effect. He has discovered how alert one must be to the ebb and flow of Marlow's narrative, and here warns the reader. But there is no single word; not even the word *trance* will do. For the shifting play of thought and feeling and image and event is very intricate. It is not vivid detail alone, the heads on stakes or the bloody shoes; nor only the dark mass of moralizing abstraction; nor the dramatized psychological intuitions apart from their context that give "Heart of Darkness" its brooding weight. The impressionist method—one cannot leave this story without subscribing to the obvious—finds here one of its great triumphs of tone. The random movement of the nightmare is also the con-

5. from "The Secret Sharer"

trolled movement of a poem, in which a quality of feeling may be stated or suggested and only much later justified. But it is justified at last. . . .

CONRAD'S TECHNIQUES: THE SYMBOLIC CIRCLE, FORESHADOWING, VIVID IMAGES, AND RHYTHMS

The narrative advances and withdraws as in a succession of long dark waves borne by an incoming tide. The waves encroach fairly evenly on the shore, and presently a few more feet of sand have been won. But an occasional wave thrusts up unexpectedly, much farther than the others: even as far, say, as Kurtz and his Inner Station. Or, to take the other figure: the flashlight is held firmly; there are no whimsical jerkings from side to side. But now and then it is raised higher, and for a brief moment in a sudden clear light we discern enigmatic matters to be explored much later. Thus the movement of the story is sinuously progressive, with much incremental repetition. The intent is not to subject the reader to multiple strains and ambiguities, but rather to throw over him a brooding gloom, such a warm pall as those two Fates in the home office might knit, back in the sepulchral city.

Yet no figure can convey "Heart of Darkness" in all its resonance and tenebrous[6] atmosphere. The movement is not one of penetration and withdrawal only; it is also the tracing of a large grand circle of awareness. It begins with the friends on the yacht under the dark above Gravesend and at last returns to them, to the tranquil waterway that "leading to the uttermost ends of the earth flowed sombre under an overcast sky—seemed to lead into the heart of an immense darkness." For this also "has been one of the dark places of the earth," and Marlow employs from the first his methods of reflexive reference and casual foreshadowing. The Romans were men enough to face this darkness of the Thames running between savage shores. "Here and there a military camp lost in a wilderness, like a needle in a bundle of hay— cold, fog, tempests, disease, exile, and death—death skulking in the air, in the water, in the bush." But these Romans were "no colonists," no more than the pilgrims of the Congo nineteen hundred years later; "their administration was merely a squeeze." Thus early Marlow establishes certain

6. dark and gloomy

political values. The French gunboat firing into a continent anticipates the blind firing of the pilgrims into the jungle when the ship has been attacked. And Marlow hears of Kurtz's first attempt to emerge from the wilderness long be fore he meets Kurtz in the flesh, and wrestles with his reluctance to leave. Marlow returns again and again, with increasing irony, to Kurtz's benevolent pamphlet.

The travelogue as travelogue is not to be ignored; and one of [British diplomat] Roger Casement's consular successors in the Congo (to whom I introduced "Heart of Darkness" in 1957) remarked at once that Conrad certainly had a "feel for the country." The demoralization of the first company station is rendered by a boiler "wallowing in the grass," by a railway truck with its wheels in the air. Presently Marlow will discover a scar in the hillside into which drainage pipes for the settlement had been tumbled; then will walk into the grove where the Negroes are free to die in a "greenish gloom." The sharply visualized particulars suddenly intrude on the somber intellectual flow of Marlow's meditation: magnified, arresting. The boilermaker who "had to crawl in the mud under the bottom of the steamboat . . . would tie up that beard of his in a kind of white serviette he brought for the purpose. It had loops to go over his ears." The papiermâché Mephistopheles is as vivid, with his delicate hooked nose and glittering mica eyes. So too is Kurtz's harlequin companion and admirer, humbly dissociating himself from the master's lusts and gratifications. "I! I! I am a simple man. I have no great thoughts." And even Kurtz, shadow and symbol though he be, the man of eloquence who in this story is almost voiceless, and necessarily so—even Kurtz is sharply visualized, an "animated image of death," a skull and body emerging as from a winding sheet, "the cage of his ribs all astir, the bones of his arm waving."

This is Africa and its flabby inhabitants; Conrad did indeed have a "feel for the country." Yet the dark tonalities and final brooding impression derive as much from rhythm and rhetoric as from such visual details: derive from the high aloof ironies and from a prose that itself advances and recedes in waves. "This initiated wraith from the back of Nowhere honored me with its amazing confidence before it vanished altogether." Or, "It is strange how I accepted this unforseen partnership, this choice of nightmares forced upon me in the tenebrous land invaded by these mean and greedy phantoms." These are true Conradian rhythms, but they are also rhythms of thought. The immediate present can be rendered with great compactness and drama: the ship staggering within ten feet of the bank at the time of the attack, and Marlow's sudden glimpse of a face amongst the leaves, then of the bush "swarming with human limbs." But still more immediate and personal, it may be, are the meditative passages evoking vast tracts of time, and the "first of men taking possession of an accursed inheritance." The prose is varied, far more so than is usual in the early work, both in rhythm and in the movements from the general to the particular and back. But the shaped sentence collecting and fully expending its breath appears to be the norm. Some of the best passages begin and end with them:

> Going up that river was like traveling back to the earliest beginnings of the world, when vegetation rioted on the earth and the big trees were kings. An empty stream, a great silence, an impenetrable forest. The air was warm, thick, heavy, sluggish. There was no joy in the brilliance of sunshine. The long stretches of the waterway ran on, deserted, into the gloom of overshadowed distances. On silvery sandbanks hippos and alligators sunned themselves side by side.

THE SIGNIFICANCE OF DARKNESS, PASSIVE AND IMMOBILE

The insistence on darkness, finally, and quite apart from ethical or mythical overtone, seems a right one for this extremely personal statement. There is a darkness of passivity, paralysis, immobilization; it is from the state of entranced languor rather than from the monstrous desires that the double Kurtz, this shadow, must be saved. In Freudian theory, we are told, such preoccupation may indicate fear of the feminine and passive. But may it not also be connected, through one of the spirit's multiple disguises, with a radical fear of death, that other darkness? "I had turned to the wilderness really, not to Mr. Kurtz, who, I was ready to admit, was as good as buried. And for a moment it seemed to me as if I also were buried in a vast grave full of unspeakable secrets. I felt an intolerable weight oppressing my breast, the smell of the damp earth, the unseen presence of victorious corruption, the darkness of an impenetrable night."

It would be folly to try to limit the menace of vegetation in the restless life of Conradian image and symbol. But the passage reminds us again of the story's reflexive references, and

its images of deathly immobilization in grass. Most striking
are the black shadows dying in the greenish gloom of the
grove at the first station. But grass sprouts between the
stones of the European city, a "whited sepulcher," and on
the same page Marlow anticipates coming upon the remains
of his predecessor: "the grass growing through his ribs was
tall enough to hide his bones." The critical meeting with
Kurtz occurs on a trail through the grass. Is there not perhaps an intense horror behind the casualness with which
Marlow reports his discoveries, say of the Negro with the
bullet in his forehead? Or: "Now and then a carrier dead in
harness, at rest in the long grass near the path, with an
empty water gourd and his long staff lying by his side."

All this, one must acknowledge, does not make up an ordinary light travelogue. There is no little irony in the letter of
November 9, 1891, Conrad received from his guardian after
returning from the Congo, and while physically disabled
and seriously depressed: "I am sure that with your melancholy temperament you ought to avoid all meditations
which lead to pessimistic conclusions. I advise you to lead a
more active life than ever and to cultivate cheerful habits."
Uneven in language on certain pages, and lacking "The Secret Sharer"'s economy, "Heart of Darkness" nevertheless
remains one of the great dark meditations in literature, and
one of the purest expressions of a melancholy temperament.

Marlow Explores the Boundaries Between Life and Death

Jeffrey Berman

According to Jeffrey Berman, Marlow's journey in *Heart of Darkness* explores death and its proximity to life. Marlow begins his journey into the Congo somewhat naive about death. Berman shows how Marlow gradually retreats from his original quest for knowledge as he learns that his survival requires him to distance himself from the symbolic wilderness and Kurtz. Berman concludes that Marlow's moral dilemma has no resolution and that his nightmare journey will continue. Jeffrey Berman has taught English at Cornell University in Ithaca, New York, and at the State University of New York at Albany. He is the author of *The Talking Cure: Literary Representations of Psychoanalysis* and *Narcissism and the Novel*.

Marlow's journey into the Congo becomes nothing less than a quest back into time for the origins and endings of man, a quest to transcend time itself and to confront the boundaries of life and death. Inherent within every quest is the element of danger, but Marlow's journey, a "weary pilgrimage amongst hints of nightmares," is fraught with so many warnings of impending catastrophes that the dangers seem less of an inevitable consequence than the actual motivating cause. We suspect that it is precisely the element of danger and the expected confrontation with death which most stimulate Marlow's curiosity to venture into Africa. Even as he sets forth all the rational reasons for his entry into the dark continent—including the desire for money and a new vocation, as well as boredom with his present life—a more powerful, irrational, force seems to impel him there. Instead of

Excerpted from *Joseph Conrad: Writing as Rescue*, by Jeffrey Berman (New York: Astra Books, 1977). Reprinted by permission of the author.

being deterred by the innumerable warnings and forbidding omens he receives about the propriety of his decision, he finds his determination only strengthened—so much so that we may feel ourselves agreeing with those in the story who question the sanity of his intentions.

Beginning with Marlow's passion for maps that echoes Conrad's autobiographical admission in *A Personal Record*— "When I grow up I will go there"—we are made aware of a preoccupation with death that borders on the obsessive. "It fascinated me as a snake would a bird—a silly little bird," Marlow admits as he gazes upon an inscrutable map of Africa in an English shop. The image subtly anticipates the long, dangerous, serpentine movement into the mouth of the Congo, from which flight or retreat becomes impossible. "The snake had charmed me," Marlow again readily confesses, unable to resist his movement toward it. Subsequent warnings serve only to accelerate the journey. The knowledge that his Danish predecessor in the Congo went berserk for no apparent reason and was killed in an absurd scuffle with the natives fails to shake Marlow's resolution, despite the fact that Fresleven was the "gentlest, quietest creature that ever walked on two legs."

Marlow's preparatory visit to the "whited sepulchre" reinforces the deadly nature of his intentions to descend into a black abyss later in the story. The singular characters he meets not only appear to be similarly preoccupied with the subject of death, but their warnings serve as part of a larger conspiracy against which Marlow finds himself helpless. The two women knitting black wool with downcast eyes look like ominous guardians of the "door of darkness," and Marlow leaves them with a wry farewell that is as self-consciously literary as it is unnaturally cheerful. "*Ave!* old knitter of black wool. *Morituri te salutant.*"[1] Later, when Marlow asks the young Company assistant why he hasn't ventured into the Congo, the latter sententiously replies, "I am not such a fool as I look, quoth [Greek philosopher] Plato to his disciples." And the doctor promptly asks him whether there was "ever any madness in your family" before enigmatically warning him to "avoid irritation more than exposure to the sun." With his best clinical detachment the doctor makes an observation which provides us with a key to

---

1. Hail! Those who are about to die salute you.

Conrad's major psychological interest in *Heart of Darkness.* "'It would be,' he said, without taking notice of my irritation, 'interesting for science to watch the mental changes of individuals, on the spot, but. . . .'" Both the doctor's ellipsis and Marlow's impatient query—"Are you an alienist"—convey a dramatic irony whose meaning does not become clear until later in the story: soon Marlow will suffer a protracted alienation from the Company, from Kurtz, and from himself.

MARLOW BEGINS HIS QUEST FOR MEANING

Only when he enters Africa does Marlow begin to unravel the grim truth underlying these persistent warnings. A well-meaning Swede, admonishing him not to continue further, narrates a seemingly minor incident that nevertheless becomes a central archetype in Conrad's fiction. "The other day I took up a man who hanged himself on the road. He was a Swede, too." "Hanged himself," Marlow exclaims with too much feigned naïveté in his tone to be entirely convincing. "Why, in God's name?" To his cry of amazement he receives only a casual shrug and an inadequate explanation: "Who knows? The sun too much for him, or the country perhaps.". . .

Only later does he recognize the lethality of his quest. As the plot of *Heart of Darkness* moves spatially from the Central Station to the Inner Station, wherein Kurtz has penetrated the surface truths of reality to the appalling inner truth associated with negation, Marlow witnesses substance deteriorating into shadow, light diminishing into darkness, sanity dissolving into madness. Underlying his suspicions that the human intellect cannot penetrate surface reality exists the deeper fear that beneath the surface lies neither order nor disorder but an absence of both conditions impossible for the imagination to comprehend. . . .

Beset everywhere by paradox and contradiction, Marlow alone possesses the subtle imagination to grasp the absurd ironies that threaten the very sanity of his complex mind. One moment he watches a man vainly trying to douse a fire by filling a pail that contains a hole in the bottom; another moment he struggles to decipher the meaning of the Russian's confusing message, "Hurry up. Approach cautiously." And after seeing Kurtz for the first time, Marlow incredulously remarks that his name, which means "short" in German, "was as true as everything else in his life—and death.

He looked at least seven feet long." The exasperation in Marlow's tone reveals a gallows humor that serves as the last defense against an indefinable force that assaults his psychic health even more than the unknown Jungle fever which later undermines his physical health.

Marlow possesses the ability, in short, to "hold two opposed ideas in the mind at the same time and still retain the ability to function.". . . He would undoubtedly agree with Robert Penn Warren's famous ambiguity in *All the King's Men*, a novel that owes much to *Lord Jim:* "The end of man is knowledge." For as Marlow painfully winds his way into the interior of the darkness, he comes to fear that the "end" or goal of man, in this case a barbarous knowledge still unknown to him, leads inseparably to the "end" or death of man.

MARLOW RETREATS FROM HIS QUEST FOR MEANING

And so while honesty compels Marlow to admit a shared affinity, however remote or repressed, to the natives howling and leaping on shore, and although elsewhere he has expressed an irritation approaching contempt toward those people "too dull" to sense the dangers surrounding them, he nevertheless backs off from discovering and participating in the fearful truths of human nature the natives embody. "You wonder I didn't go ashore for a howl and a dance? Well, no— I didn't. Fine sentiments, you say? Fine sentiments, be hanged! I had no time. I had to mess about with white-lead and strips of woollen blanket helping to put bandages on those leaky steam-pipes—I tell you. I had to watch the steering, and circumvent those snags, and get the tin-pot along by hook or by crook. There was surface-truth enough in these things to save a wiser man." In *Lord Jim* the older and more subdued Marlow declares, speaking from undisclosed personal experience, "No man ever understands quite his own artful dodges to escape from the grim shadow of self-knowledge." We wonder whether the Marlow of *Heart of Darkness* realizes that during key moments of his narrative he, too, resorts to artful dodging to escape from in this case deadly self-knowledge. The combination of defensiveness and belligerence in his voice, together with his grateful reliance upon busy work to nurse an over-active imagination back to normalcy, point to the conclusion that for the first though by no means for the last time in *Heart of Darkness*

Marlow finds himself retreating from the goal of self-discovery that has initially prompted him into the Congo. Again and again Marlow's moments of greatest imaginative vision compel him out of the necessity of self-preservation to avert his eyes to what finally defeats Kurtz. Not only does the process of expansion and contraction of consciousness roughly coincide with Marlow's serpentine movement up the river toward Kurtz, but it also constitutes the scene-by-scene construction of the novella. Repeatedly Marlow's curiosity projects him into situations in which he glimpses new possibilities of experience. To "know" these experiences, which has been part of Marlow's original aim in undertaking his quest, apparently requires full participation within them, whether it be joining the natives in their unearthly dances or sharing in Kurtz's unspeakable rites. But even as Marlow finds himself dangerously drawn toward these experiences and their incarnate dark knowledge, he prudently holds back before it is too late, thus making possible his continued survival.

Marlow's most frequent method of retreat is the escape into work, either the mindless riveting of the steamer's torn hull or the simple devotion to detail involved in steering the ship. At first he misleadingly refers to work as if it were conducive to self-discovery. "No, I don't like work. I had rather laze about and think of all the fine things that can be done. I don't like work—no man does—but I like what is in the work—the chance to find yourself." A few pages later he contradicts himself by admitting that work happily impedes the process of self-discovery. "When you have to attend to things of that sort, to the mere incidents of the surface, the reality—the reality, I tell you—fades. The inner truth is hidden—luckily, luckily." Insofar as work slows the introspective voyage by serving as a brake against the accelerating descent into the self, it becomes nothing less than the central method of self-therapy in Conrad's universe. Work becomes as much a moral imperative and psychic restorative as it becomes a physical activity; even if the work accomplishes nothing materially, it remains a life-saving illusion without which we could not exist. Marlow's insistent demand for rivets has the literal meaning of repairing the steamer's gaping hull; but it also has the larger symbolic meaning of investing substance into hollowness. Starch has a similar literal and symbolic effect. By adding firmness to limp body, it creates a self-preservative form against the formlessness of the jungle. Hence Marlow's inordinate admiration for the starched collars of the Company's chief accountant. "In the great demoralization of the land kept up his appearance. That's backbone. His starched collars and got-up shirt-fronts were achievements of character." Admittedly only surface truths, these symbols of work and order comprise man's last embattled defense against the assaulting dark powers. As the Marlow of *Chance* shrewdly observes, "to be busy with material affairs is the best preservative against reflection, fears, doubts—all these things which stand in the way of achievement. . . .

THE DILEMMA OF LOYALTY TO KURTZ

In short, Conrad has ensnared Marlow in a psycho-moral dilemma that proves insoluble to the best rational analysis. Loyalty to Kurtz implies for Marlow a permanent surrender to the nightmarish vision which appalls the imagination and culminates in "The horror! The horror!" But disloyalty to Kurtz, in this case the simple effort that is by no means simple to avoid plunging into the abyss, awakens in the man of conscience a twin failure: an intellectual failure which derives from the abandonment of his quest for final knowledge, and the sense of human failure which arises from the guilt felt by the survivor of a catastrophe that has been fatal to his friend. That this "disloyalty" is entirely self-defined and self-perceived matters little; nor does it matter that the "crime" is necessary for one's self-preservation. The psychic effect is the same as if one committed a less subjective "betrayal.". . .

As he affirms to the Manager of the Central Station his reluctant loyalty to Kurtz, whom he now considers "as good as buried," he experiences one of those epiphany-like visions which irrevocably alter one's conception of the world. "And for a moment it seemed to me as if I also were buried in a vast grave full of unspeakable secrets. I felt an intolerable weight oppressing my breast, the smell of the damp earth, the unseen presence of victorious corruption, the darkness of an impenetrable night. . . ."

To resist this fatal hold Marlow finds himself implicated in an experience so bizarre and yet so archetypal that not even his carefully wrought retrospective narration can fully comprehend its meaning. Awakening at midnight to discover that

Kurtz has crawled out of the hut to rejoin the natives, Marlow suffers a shock that forever renders absurd his once heroic efforts to converse with the man whose genius for expression has enlarged the minds of others. A new image of Marlow emerges, that of a man compelled to exorcise the nightmare called Kurtz. But Conrad does not use the metaphor of exorcism: he uses language whose violence is less rhetorical than it is both literal and immediate, suggestive of a man barely able to restrain himself from an inner rage that threatens to explode outward in the form of homicide. Finding himself crawling along the grass in a manner reminiscent of Kurtz, Marlow makes an admission that becomes even more convincing because of his tense body and desperate tone. "I strode rapidly with clenched fists. I fancy I had some vague notion of falling upon him and giving him a drubbing. I don't know. I had some imbecile thoughts." And when Kurtz vainly tries to begin the long-awaited dialogue by murmuring in a tone faltering between tragedy and pathos, "I had immense plans," Marlow brutally cuts him off. " 'Yes,' said I; 'but if you try to shout I'll smash your head with—.' " After delivering additional threats, Marlow drags Kurtz back to the cabin in a coldly impersonal manner, suggestive of another desperate retreat into the therapeutic mindlessness of work. Thus ends their only recorded encounter. Shortly after Marlow's abandonment of him, Kurtz dies, and the close chronological connection implies a causal relationship. To the other men of the steamer, Marlow's conspicuous refusal to mourn or even to take an interest in his death betrays a sharp contradiction of the intense loyalty he once expressed toward Kurtz. "All the pilgrims rushed out to see" Kurtz's death; "I remained, and went on with my dinner. I believe I was considered brutally callous.". . .

MARLOW'S ILLNESS AND SURVIVAL

The close proximity of Kurtz's death to the approach of Marlow's sudden and equally inexplicable illness suggests the kind of ritualized penance to which Conrad's characters must submit themselves after a morally ambiguous action. After the others unceremoniously bury Kurtz into a muddy hole "they very nearly buried me," Marlow notes with a wryness that comes only from retrospection. "However, as you see, I did not go to join Kurtz there and then. I did not. I remained to dream the nightmare out to the end, and to show my loyalty to Kurtz once more." If the syntax associates Marlow's "loyalty" to Kurtz with the eventual recovery of his own health, the subsequent events of the story together with the worsening of his nightmare imply that his belated loyalty to the dead man now demands an even more active continuation of the horror, to the point of joining him in death. And this is what almost occurs: "I have wrestled with death. It is the most unexciting contest you can imagine. It takes place in an impalpable grayness, with nothing underfoot, with nothing around, without spectators, without clamour, without glory, without the great desire of victory, without the great fear of defeat, in a sickly atmosphere of tepid scepticism, without much belief in your own right, and still less in that of your adversary." Although the metaphor of wrestling suggests an active, locatable assailant, Marlow appears more endangered by apathy, listlessness, a drying up of the will to live. . . .

Throughout *Heart of Darkness* Marlow's imagination has been baffled by codes he cannot decipher, clues he cannot interpret, cries of horror he cannot silence. Survival itself becomes the insoluble enigma, the first question he invariably ponders whenever he encounters a new figure, dead or alive. Significantly, most of the figures he comes across are either dead or dying. Thus his efforts to decipher the enigmatic expression on the face of the dying helmsman. "I declare it looked as though he would presently put to us some question in an understandable language; but he died without uttering a sound, without moving a limb, without twitching a muscle." Kurtz has rephrased the dying helmsman's question into statement form—or more precisely, into the form of a piercing cry: "The horror! The horror!" Fresleven, the hanged Swede, the shrunken heads "smiling continuously at some endless and jocose dream of that external slumber"—all seem to hold mysterious answers that serve only to mock the futility of Marlow's questions.

"I was within a hair's breadth of the last opportunity for pronouncement, and I found with humiliation that probably I would have nothing to say." Unwilling to dismiss the affirmative value of Kurtz's intolerably intense vision that is wide enough to embrace both the heights and depths of existence, Marlow himself has reached—imaginatively and morally—a dead end. Reluctantly rejecting his former great expectations of discovering a pattern that will somehow unlock the secrets of life and death, he is left to mull over in his imagination the subject that has left him speechless in the jungle. . . .

MARLOW'S CONTINUING ANGUISH

Nor does Marlow's anguish cease when he utters the justly famous "true lie" to Kurtz's Intended. The lie, however compassionate and paradoxical, nevertheless represents to Marlow an appalling self-degradation that causes him to shrink in moral revulsion. . . . Conrad places Marlow in another impossible moral dilemma, one involving, quite simply, a choice between a pitiless truth that would no doubt crush the idealistic Intended or a compassionate lie that would forever haunt Marlow's conscience. Unable to find solace in the paradox that in this case wisdom and humanity together reside in the fabrication of an illusion, Marlow—"with a dull anger stirring in me"—makes his fateful choice, fully aware of the implications of the most momentous sacrifice of his life. As he informs her that Kurtz's last words were "your name," an exultant cry escapes her lips; but Conrad, unable to forgive her for the victory she has achieved at the expense of the man wavering in front of her, already has shifted his major interest to the grim struggle silently raging within Marlow. For now, Kurtz's last words ironically thunder through him as he finds his imagination involuntarily projected back into the heart of darkness. Menacing whispers of "The horror! The horror!" now crash through the room; an image of a vengeful Kurtz appears before him, angry at the "justice which was his due." And now Marlow's distinctions between loyalty and betrayal become hopelessly entangled; the final betrayal of Kurtz's demand for justice serves to heighten the "taint of death," the "flavour of mortality," that symbolically reunites Marlow with the dead man. Marlow lives, of course, to finish the narration of his story; but the story itself reenacts a horror that has no finish for him. Like [Romantic poet Samuel Taylor] Coleridge's Ancient Mariner, Marlow is fated to tell his story again and again, compelled in the process to suffer and experience a loss of life. As *Heart of Darkness* concludes with a blackening sky and the resumption of the meditating Buddha pose, we sense that Marlow's nightmare has only begun.

Marlow Gains Insight Through Work

Ted E. Boyle

Ted E. Boyle interprets Marlow's physical labor as a
bridge between his first dark impressions of the
jungle and his transformation into a mythic hero
with a mission. Boyle argues that through work
Marlow and his native helmsman create a bond, the
awareness of which opens Marlow to new discoveries. Ted E. Boyle has been an instructor in English
at Kansas State University in Manhattan and at
Southern Illinois University in Carbondale. He has
contributed critical articles to professional journals
on Joseph Conrad, Catherine Mansfield, E.M.
Forster, William Golding, and Kingsley Amis.

Conrad's method in "Heart of Darkness", as in all his best
work, is exceedingly complex. In fact, he sustains three distinct patterns of imagery in this tale, first emphasizing one,
then another, and finally uniting all three in the brilliantly
conceived final scene. In the section of the narrative which
begins with Marlow's accepting the job as captain of the
"twopenny steamer" and ends with his starting to repair the
sunken wreck of the ship, the imagery and symbolism center on the black futility which Marlow feels in his own soul,
and on his initiation into a knowledge of the horrible small-
ness of mankind. In the section of the story which starts
with Marlow's repairing the steamer and continues through
the death of his helmsman, the dominant imagery focuses
on work as a saving grace. When Marlow meets Kurtz, the
emphasis is again shifted. At this point Marlow becomes a
sort of mythic hero whose task is to discover a beneficent
talisman which will aid all mankind. These systems of imagery are by no means mutually exclusive. Images of darkness occur in all three sections. Even as Marlow concentrates

Excerpted from *Symbol and Meaning in the Fiction of Joseph Conrad*, by Ted E. Boyle
(The Hague: Mouton, 1965). Reprinted by permission of Mouton de Gruyter, a division
of Walter de Gruyter GmbH & Co., Berlin and New York.

on his work as ship's captain in section two, it is evident he is already engaged in a sort of mythic quest. In section three the symbolism emphasizes Marlow's discovery and his return with the restorative boon, yet work imagery is an ever-present undertone. . . .

WORK SAVES MARLOW FROM THE DARKNESS

After his dark experiences in the grove of death and his meeting with the weak, greedy pilgrims, Marlow nearly loses his faith in the redeeming idea at the back of the colonial operation. The horror of his experiences has driven him ever deeper into his own consciousness, and he nearly falls into that everlasting deep hole in which even honor, courage, and honest devotion to duty seem hollow. Kurtz strikes out in blind, revengeful egoism because he can discern no system of order in the elemental jungle, the passive stupidity of its black inhabitants, or the disguised avarice of the colonial enterprise. In the face of this enormous stupidity, why should an intelligent man not make his own laws?

Through work Marlow is saved from the spiritual disintegration to which unrestrained egoism leads. The job of repairing the battered steamer permits him "to come out a bit", to immerse the morbidity of his self-consciousness in some fixed value outside himself:

> No, I don't like work. I had rather laze about and think of all the fine things that can be done. I don't like work—no man does—but I like what is in the work,—the chance to find yourself. Your own reality—for yourself, not for others—what no other man can ever know. They can only see the mere show, and never can tell what it really means.

Certainly Marlow's work is more than a device to retain his sanity. This is clearly seen when his devotion to duty is compared with that of the chief accountant at the first station. The accountant substitutes starched shirts and faultlessly kept account books for being human. His work makes him stop asking questions, makes him stop searching for a meaning in the absurd jumble of noble ideas, white men, jungle, disease, black men, and death. Marlow's work, however, offers him a secure position from which he can continue his quest for the redeeming idea, the small grain of truth which he is sure exists even in the depths of the Congo. His work is not a retreat but an opening out.

THE SIGNIFICANCE OF THE BRICK-MAKER
AND THE BOILER-MAKER

At the Central Station Marlow sees the degeneration of men who have no object in life except the accumulation of wealth, but now that he has firmly anchored himself in his work, they do not cause him to despair so much. He can observe that their lack of any unselfish objective, not the illogic of the universe, accounts for their inhumanity. The station's brick-maker symbolizes the plight of all the pilgrims. He is apparently not an altogether unpromising young man, but deprived of any possibility of fulfilling his job of making bricks, he turns into a spy for the station manager. Marlow describes him as a papier-maché Mephistopheles and comments ironically on his moral weakness:

> The business intrusted to this fellow was the making of bricks—so I had been informed; but there wasn't a fragment of a brick anywhere in the station, and he had been there more than a year—waiting. It seems he could not make bricks without something, I don't know what—straw maybe. Anyways, it could not be found there, and as it was not likely to be sent from Europe, it did not appear clear to me what he was waiting for. An act of special creation perhaps.

The brick-maker needs straw, and Marlow needs rivets. He has sufficient plates to cover the holes in the side of the ancient steamer, but he has no rivets, and the station manager is not particularly disposed to get him any. Rivets become an obsession with Marlow. He dreams of the wealth of rivets at the first station:

> You kicked a loose rivet at every second step in that station yard on the hillside. Rivets had rolled into the grove of death. You could fill your pockets with rivets for the trouble of stooping down—and there wasn't one rivet to be found where it was wanted.

In his conversation with the brick-maker, who apparently has some influence with the station manager, Marlow demands rivets. When he and the boiler-maker with whom he has been working are confident that they shall, indeed, have some rivets, they dance a grotesque jig on the deck of the steamer. Rivets have clearly become to Marlow a symbol of the redeeming ideas of civilization, the ideas of humanity and solidarity which enable man to constrain hostile nature: "What I wanted was a certain quantity of rivets—and rivets were what really Mr. Kurtz wanted, if he had only known it".

It is also significant that in order to obtain rivets for his ship, Marlow goes "near enough to a lie". When the brick-maker overestimates the importance of Marlow's connections in Europe, Marlow does not correct him. The brick-maker apparently reports that this influential man wants rivets desperately, and the station manager has them sent. Marlow's first "lie", then, enables him, if the symbolic significance of the rivets is accepted, to gain access to the strength which he must have to front the elemental evil which would turn him into a scheming animal. His second "lie" is of much the same nature.

Slowly, Marlow, though never ignoring the ever-present danger which the jungle represents, begins to see order where before he could see only chaos. There is a certain fitness in the boiler-maker's tying up his waist-length beard in a serviette to keep it clean as he crawls in the mud underneath the ship repairing her. He immerses himself in the destructive element, the river's primeval ooze, but by the force of his imagination he keeps a part of himself clean.

THE RITUAL OF WORK PROVIDES PROTECTION

When Marlow gets the ship underway, he travels further yet into the heart of darkness. During this part of his voyage, the exercise of his craft becomes even more important to the maintenance of his spiritual sanity, for now he realizes that he possesses a heritage in common with the savages whom he sees on the river banks:

> It was unearthly, and the men were—No, they were not inhuman. Well, you know, that was the worst of it—this suspicion of their not being inhuman. It would come slowly to one. They howled and leaped and spun, and made horrid faces; but what thrilled you was just the thought of their humanity —like yours—the thought of your remote kinship with the wild and passionate uproar. Ugly. Yes, it was ugly enough; but if you were man enough you would admit to yourself that there was in you just the faintest trace of a response to the terrible frankness of that noise, a dim suspicion of there being a meaning in it which you—you so remote from the night of first ages—could comprehend.

Yet, since he is protected from the primeval ugliness by the ritual of his work, he can begin to discern the truth for which he is searching:

> What was there after all? Joy, fear, sorrow, devotion, valour, rage—who can tell?—but truth—truth stripped of its cloak of

time. . . . You wonder I didn't go ashore for a howl and a dance? Well, no—I didn't. Fine sentiments, you say? Fine sentiments, be hanged! I had no time. I had to mess about with white-lead and strips of woollen blanket helping to put bandages on those leaky steam-pipes—I tell you. I had to watch the steering, and circumvent those snags, and get the tin-pot along by hook or by crook. There was a surface-truth enough in these things to save a wiser man.

In his fireman and his cannibal crew, Marlow reads the story of mankind's faltering and painful journey out of the dark jungle. The fireman tends the boiler with assiduous care because he believes that if he lets the water fall below a certain mark on the gauge, the spirit inside the boiler will become angry and devour him. He does not understand his work, but he is useful to the ship, and the knowledge of the ship's operation which he possesses is "improving knowledge".

It is an indication of how far Marlow has pierced into the heart of darkness that his not being eaten by a fellow human being is to him a hopeful sign. It is also a tribute to Conrad's ability to present the primary, unadorned realities of existence that, in describing the cannibal's restraint, he gives an infinitely more meaningful perspective on the solidarity of mankind than can volumes of preaching about the brotherhood of man. The cannibals have no inherited experience to teach them a code of behaviour. They do not understand the contract under which they are bound, and their pay—three pieces of brass wire a month—is useless to them. They are hungry, but yet they perform their duties and apparently never think of dining on Marlow and the pilgrims. Marlow jokes that he, if he were a cannibal, would not eat the pilgrims either—they are unwholesome in any sense of the word—but he is mystified by the cannibals' restraint:

> Restraint! What possible restraint? Was it superstition, disgust, patience, fear—or some kind of primitive honour? No fear can stand up to hunger, no patience can wear it out, disgust simply does not exist where hunger is; and as to superstition, beliefs, and what you may call principles, they are less than chaff in a breeze.

Marlow sees that the nobility of the human spirit is in fact a greater mystery than the nameless brute thing waiting in the jungle:

> But there was the fact facing me—the fact dazzling, to be seen, like the foam on the depths of the sea, like a ripple on an unfathomable enigma, a mystery greater—when I thought of it—than the curious, inexplicable note of desperate grief in

this savage clamour that had swept by us on the river-bank, behind the blind whiteness of the fog.

He is beginning to fit the facts of his experience into some meaningful pattern, and Conrad skilfully guides the reader along the path of Marlow's ever-more-hopeful quest.

WORK ENABLES MARLOW TO FIND VALUE AND SYMPATHY

One of the most effective symbols in this, the second section of "Heart of Darkness", is the tattered book, *An Inquiry into Some Points of Seamanship*. Marlow, when he discovers this volume in the deserted hut of the Russian harlequin, can be said to be almost cheerful:

> Not a very enthralling book; but at the first glance you could see there a singleness of intention, an honest concern for the right way of going to work, which made these humble pages, thought out so many years ago, luminous with another than a professional light. The simple old sailor, with his talk of chains and purchases, made me forget the jungle and the pilgrims in a delicious sensation of having come upon something unmistakably real.

He has in his hands at last a tangible manifestation of the honor which he has been able to salvage from the chaos of Africa.

Marlow's devotion to his work is a code which enables him to find value in life. In fact, some twenty years before [American writer Ernest] Hemingway began to write, Conrad had conceived in the Marlow of "Heart of Darkness" the "code hero". Cayetano, Harry Wilson, the "non-messy" people in *The Sun Also Rises,* and old Santiago are direct descendants of Marlow. Perhaps their code is a bit narrower, and perhaps it allows them to come out of themselves a bit less, yet Hemingway's characters who are true to the code must, like Marlow, "breathe dead hippo and not be contaminated". . . .

Conrad blends the first and second parts of the story together by bringing the work imagery to the fore just at the moment when Marlow seems to have lost all faith in making his mind triumph over the futility which he observes around him. The second section of the story flows perfectly into the third section, in which the emphasis is on Marlow as mythic hero, in the scene in which Marlow's helmsman is killed. Here Marlow's work ethic enables him to come even further out of himself. He acknowledges his personal tie to his helmsman, and, in a blood ritual, purges himself of the heritage of guilt which his predecessor Fresleven has left him. [Critic] Lillian Feder, in tracing the parallels between Marlow's descent into the underworld and that of [Roman poet Virgil's] Aeneas, likens Marlow's helmsman to Aeneas's Palinurus, and certainly there is ample evidence that these two helmsmen fulfil generally the same function in their respective stories.

The Sibyl tells Aeneas:

> "make
> Sacrifice of black sheep: only when you are thus
> Purified, shall you see the Stygian groves and the regions
> Not visible to the living."

Marlow's helmsman seems to be his master's "black sheep".

However, when Feder says that "both die 'insontes'" (guiltless), and loyal to their leaders, she seemingly overlooks an important difference between Palinurus and Marlow's helmsman. Palinurus slips and falls accidentally into the sea, but is so intent on his job of steering that he holds to the tiller even as he falls and carries it with him. Marlow's helmsman leaves the tiller and throws open the shutter of the deck house to fire a rifle at the natives on the bank. He does not die guiltless; he has failed in his duty. Like the helmsman of the "Narcissus" who left his post during the near mutiny, Marlow's helmsman has been overcome by the evil, insidious powers which abhor solidarity. The helmsman's death, which comes as a direct result of his leaving the wheel, is Conrad's symbolic comment on the wages of dereliction of duty. Kurtz has also, in a sense, left the tiller.

The death of the helmsman fulfils additional important symbolic functions. As has been previously noted, when the native falls dead at Marlow's feet, Marlow realizes that his work has enabled him to understand and sympathize with a fellow human being. The helmsman is by no means proficient at his job, but Marlow perceives that there is something mystic and profoundly human about this native's imperfect attempts to steer the ship when it would be more reasonable for him to be ashore howling and dancing. Marlow is a nineteenth-century Englishman, and Conrad never allows him to express views inconsistent with the "idea at the back" of Victorian colonial policy. The Negroes of the Congo have been represented to Marlow by his society as an inferior species of human being; thus, he feels almost defensive as he expresses his sympathy for one:

I missed my late helmsman awfully,—I missed him even while his body was still lying in the pilot-house. Perhaps you will think it passing strange this regret for a savage who was no more account than a grain of sand in a black Sahara. Well, don't you see, he had done something, he had steered; for months I had him at my back—a help—an instrument. It was a kind of partnership. He steered for me—I had to look after him, I worried about his deficiencies, and thus a subtle bond had been created, of which I only became aware when it was suddenly broken.

The solidarity of mankind, Marlow realizes, does not rest on the irrelevancies of skin color. The sympathy which Marlow gains for his helmsman through the ritual of work has enabled him to identify with the soul of black Africa as Kurtz, with all the eloquence of his seventeen page pamphlet, never could.

Conrad Pioneers New Themes and Methods

Frederick R. Karl

Frederick R. Karl praises *Heart of Darkness* as a great novel. He cites it as a pioneering psychological and visionary investigation into twentieth-century politics and morality. Moreover, according to Karl, Conrad creates artistic methods to engage the reader intellectually and emotionally in profound moral issues. Frederick R. Karl has taught English at New York University. He is the author of *The Adversary Literature: The English Novel in the Eighteenth Century* and a standard biography, *Joseph Conrad: The Three Lives*, and is coeditor of the multivolume collection of Conrad's letters.

Heart of Darkness is possibly the greatest short novel in English and is one of the greatest in any language. Like all great fiction, it involves the reader in dramatic, crucially difficult moral decisions which parallel those of the central characters. It asks troublesome questions, disturbs preconceptions, forces curious confrontations, and possibly changes us. With one of the two central characters, Kurtz, we sense the allure of great power. With the other, Marlow, we edge toward an abyss and return different. . . .

CONRAD, LIKE FREUD, IS A PIONEER IN PSYCHOLOGICAL EXPLORATION

It [*Heart of Darkness*] contains also that which [psychoanalyst] Sigmund Freud suggests may be found in his own *Interpretation of Dreams*, namely an insight that falls to one but once in a lifetime. The reference to Freud and to *Dreams* is not fortuitous. It was of course chance that Freud and Conrad were contemporaries, but chance ends when we note the extraordinary parallelism of their achievements. Freud did his

From Frederick R. Karl, "Introduction to the Danse Macabre: Conrad's *Heart of Darkness*," *Modern Fiction Studies*, vol. 14 (1968), pp. 143–56. Copyright © 1968, Purdue Research Foundation. Reprinted by permission of the Johns Hopkins University Press.

major work on dreams in the 1890s, the same time that Conrad was fermenting ideas about the Congo and personal and political expedience in a quicksand, nightmarish world. Freud's book, the culmination of his observations, appeared in 1900, only months after Conrad's *Heart of Darkness.* Chance is further reduced when we recognize that literature and a new style of psychological exploration have been first cousins for more than a hundred years, that both Conrad and Freud were pioneers in stressing the irrational elements in human behavior which resisted orthodox interpretation. Conrad's great contribution to political thought is his insight into the irrationality of politics, its nightmarish qualities which depend on the neurosis of a leader, in turn upon the collective neuroses of a people. Such an insight is timeless, but it is particularly helpful to those of us seeking to understand historical developments since 1900. For when has humankind tried so carefully to preserve life while also squandering it so carelessly? Conrad caught not only hypocrisy (an old-fashioned value) but the illogic of human behavior which tries to justify itself with precision, only to surrender to explosive inner needs. "Exterminate all the brutes," Kurtz scrawled at the bottom of his report. This is the politics of personal disintegration, uncontrollable personal needs, ultimately paranoia.

Confronting similar material, the scientist Freud was concerned to analyze logically the seeming illogic, the apparent irrationality, of dreams and, on occasion, of nightmares. Both he and Conrad penetrated into the darkness, the darkness entered into when people sleep or when their consciences sleep, when they are free to pursue secret wishes, whether in dreams, like Freud's analysands, or in actuality, like Kurtz and his followers. The key word is *darkness*; the black of the jungle for Conrad is the dark of the sleeping consciousness for Freud.

In still another sense, Marlow, in his trip up the Congo, has suffered through a nightmare, an experience that sends him back a different man, now aware of depths in himself that he cannot hide. . . .

Marlow, however, only barely restrains himself, for, irresistibly, he is drawn toward Kurtz, readily accepting the latter's ruthlessness as preferable to the bland hypocrisy of the station manager. Even Marlow is seduced—he, too, hides secret wishes and desires, his dreams curiously close to

Kurtz's; and so are the dreams of us all, Conrad suggests. Kurtz's savage career is every man's wish-fulfillment, although by dying he conveniently disappears before we all become his disciples.

CONRAD CONFRONTS TROUBLING MORAL ISSUES

But *not* before we are filled with a sense of the absurd—a sense of the absurd gap between what we profess to be and what we are, a sense of our consequently and inevitably skewed relationship with objects, with our milieu, with the universe itself. . . .

In a letter to [writer and friend] Cunninghame Graham, written while *Heart of Darkness* was welling up in 1898, Conrad reveals his most personal fears: that in a world of ever-shifting illusions nothing, finally, matters and no one, ultimately, cares:

> In a dispassionate view the ardour for reform, improvement for virtue, for knowledge, and even for beauty is only a vain sticking up for appearances as though one were anxious about the cut of one's clothes in a community of blind men. Life knows us not and we do not know life—we don't know even our own thoughts. Half the words we use have no meaning whatever and of the other half each man understands each word after the fashion of his own folly and conceit. Faith is a myth and beliefs shift like mists on the shore; thoughts vanish; words, once pronounced, die; and the memory of yesterday is as shadowy as the hope of to-morrow—only the string of my platitudes seems to have no end. As our [Polish] peasants say: "Pray, brother, forgive me for the love of God." And we don't know what forgiveness is, nor what is love, nor where God is. Assez.[1]

Heart of Darkness, then, is concerned with moral issues in their most troubling sense: not only as philosophical imperatives, but practically as they work out in human behavior.

CONRAD'S IMAGES AND SYMBOLS

In another letter to Cunninghame Graham, written a year later, Conrad seems less to reflect philosophically than to discuss the sources of his imagery. He stresses apropos of *Heart of Darkness* that he didn't start "with an abstract notion" but with "definite images." Such images abound: from the ludicrous French gunboat to its shells lobbed indiscriminately into the bush, then the metal of nuts and bolts and de-

---

1. enough

caying, overturned equipment, the rusted steamboat settled in the mud, even the polished, unnatural accountant at the station, with the land itself silhouetted by withered natives, shades of themselves, victims of an imperialist Inferno, now dried, inhuman, lacking flesh or spirit, too soft for modern life. These definite images, however, suggest moral issues, as well as a philosophical position. The profusion of metallic and mechanical images indicates that resistant objects have superseded softness, flexibility, humanity itself; that, clearly, one must become an object, tough and durable, in order to survive.

The sense of human waste that pervades the story is best unfolded in the smoothly metallic, white luxurious ivory itself. It is an object for the rich—in decorations, for piano keys, for bibelots[2]—hardly necessary for physical or mental survival. In a way, it is like art, a social luxury, and it is for art that the Congo is plundered and untold numbers slaughtered brutally, or casually. This view of ivory as art was surely part of Conrad's conception; a utilitarian object would have had its own *raison d'être*.[3] A relatively useless item or one selective in its market only points up the horror; surely this, too, is part of Kurtz's vision. Possibly Kurtz's artistic propensities (he paints, he collects human heads, he seeks ivory) make him so contemptuous of individual lives; for art and life have always warred. In the name of art (pyramids, churches, tombs, monuments, palaces), how many have died, gone without, worked as slaves? Traditionally, beauty for the few is gained with blood of the many. . . .

Kurtz has risen above the masses—of natives, station managers, even of directors back in Brussels. He must continue to assert himself, a megalomaniac in search of further power. Marlow has never met anyone like him, this Kurtz who represents all of Europe. The insulated Englishman now faces east, toward the continent. "I took great care to give a cosmopolitan origin to Kurtz," Conrad noted in a 1903 letter to [writer and friend Kazimierz] Waliszewski. "All Europe contributed to the making of Kurtz," we read.

He is indeed Europe, searching for power, maneuvering for advantage; and he finds the lever in the colonial adventure of ivory. No wonder, then, that Kurtz's hunger for acquisition is so overwhelming. Supremacy over all is all he

2. trinkets 3. reason for existence

seeks: supremacy over things, people, and, finally, values. Having gratified forbidden desires, he is free of civilized taboos. In the Congo, he can do anything. His only prescription: produce results, send back ivory. Indeed, his very will to power and confident brutality make him appear a kind of god to the natives and other agents who fear him and to the Russian sailor who believes in him.

The ultimate corruption is that Kurtz can go his way without restraint. All human barriers are down. Only power counts—no matter whether political or economic. In the jungle, as in enterprise, only the strong survive, and Kurtz obviously is one of the strong. . . .

KURTZ REPRESENTS MODERN SOCIAL AND POLITICAL VALUES

The absence of social morality, the desire to rise at everyone's expense, the manipulation of whole peoples for purely selfish ends, the obsession with image and consensus, and personal power, the absence of meaningful beliefs, the drive for advancement and aggrandizement without larger considerations, the career built on manipulation and strategies, not ideas: these are the traits that have characterized the leaders of our age, that have become the expected burden of the ruled in our century. The rapists have been Belgian, German, Russian, and American—though they have, to be sure, raped and plundered in different ways and to varying degrees. Too often power is vested in the chameleon, the politician who claims to be all things to all people. "The best lack all conviction," as [Irish poet] William Butler Yeats expresses it in "The Second Coming," "while the worst are full of passionate intensity."

In this conception of Kurtz Conrad's powers as an artistic thinker were at their strongest. In reading Conrad it is often necessary to discriminate between pure thought and thought embodied in a work of art. As a political and social theorist, he was antagonistic to modern developments, deeply conservative in the sense that he suspected or mocked new departures or experiments. As an artistic thinker, however, he was at once caustic, subtle, broad. . . .

Conrad was concerned with the rape of a people. The Congo had been, since 1875, the private preserve of Leopold II of Belgium, a medieval kingdom for personal use, organized under the deceptive title of the International Association for the Civilization of Central Africa. Demographists estimate that hundreds of thousands, possibly millions, of Congolese died in slavery or through brutality. Kurtz, or his type of exploiter, was the rule, not the exception. Kurtz himself was based roughly and loosely on one Georges-Antoine Klein (Klein = small, Kurtz = short), whom Conrad had taken aboard his steamer during his Congo days. Conrad's journey, as he relates in his Congo diary, was real; Kurtz and his type prevailed; the land and the natives existed; the facts are undisputed. Even if Conrad used symbols to excess, as he feared, each symbol is solidly grounded in fact. Here is white against black, entrenched against primitive, have against have-not, machine against spear, civilization against tribe.

INTERPRETATIONS OF KURTZ'S FINAL WORDS

If Conrad's novella is to have artistic as well as political significance, it must make broad reference to human motivation and behavior. One evident part of the application comes with Kurtz's double shriek of "The horror! The horror!" The cry is far richer and more ambiguous than most readers make it. We must remember that Marlow is reporting, and Marlow has a particular view and need of Kurtz. As Marlow understands the scream, it represents a moral victory; that is, on the threshold of death, Kurtz has reviewed his life with all its horror and in some dying part of him has repented. Marlow hears the words as a victory of moral sensibility over a life of brutality and prostituted ideals. This "Christian" reading of the words is, of course, what Marlow himself wishes to hear; he is a moral man, and he believes, with this kind of bourgeois religiosity, that all men ultimately repent when confronted by the great unknown. Kurtz's cry, in this interpretation, fits in with what Marlow wants to know of human nature.

We are not all Marlows, however, and we should not be seduced into agreeing with him, even if he is partially right. More ambiguously and ironically, Kurtz's cry might be a shriek of despair that after having accomplished so little he must now perish. His horror is the anguish of one who dies with his work incomplete. In this view, Kurtz does not repent; rather, he bewails a fate which frustrates his plans. Indeed, at the very moment of death, he challenges life and death and tries to make his baffled will prevail. Like Satan in [British poet John] Milton's *Paradise Lost*, he prefers hell to compromise.

Just because Marlow fails to see Kurtz as a devil, however, does not mean that his author did. Conrad always harked back to the individual devil in each man—perhaps as part of his Catholic background. He believed that men deceived themselves to the very end: about the evil in others and in themselves. "Our refuge is in stupidity, in drunkenness of all kinds, in lies, in beliefs, in murder, thieving, reforming—in negation, in contempt," he wrote in 1898, in yet another letter to Cunninghame Graham. "There is no morality, no knowledge and no hope; there is only the consciousness of ourselves which drives us about a world that whether seen in a convex or a concave mirror is always but a vain and floating appearance."

Marlow cannot, or will not, admit the truth of what Conrad here suggests. Returning from the world of the dead, Marlow—our twentieth-century Everyman—cannot even admit the full impact of the indecency he has witnessed, of the feelings he has experienced. Even this most honest of men must disguise what he has seen and felt. Like a politician he must bed down with lies. Marlow, that pillar of truth and morality, does Kurtz's work at the end, lies to protect the lie of Kurtz's existence, ultimately lies to preserve his (Marlow's) own illusions. In an impure, dirty world, he desperately seeks a compromise—and finds it in the pretty illusions of naive women. Only Conrad, who is outside both Marlow and Kurtz, can admit the truth, can limn the lie and see it as a lie. Only the artist, and his art, can triumph; all else is dragged down or forced to exist by virtue of untruths. Marlow, the narrator, controlled in turn by Conrad, the creator, can transform the horror of his experience into the human terms necessary for continued life. Conrad has succeeded in constructing a form which can, so to speak, hold the horror at arm's length and yet also touch us deeply. . . .

SETTING, STRUCTURE, AND METHOD
UNITE LANGUAGE AND IDEAS

The jungle itself, that vast protective camouflage barring the light of sun and sky, masks and hides, becoming part of the psychological as well as physical landscape. Like the dream content, it forms itself around distortion, condensation, and displacement. Post-Darwinian and overpowering, the jungle is not Wordsworth's gentle landscape, by no means the type of nature which gives strength and support in our darkest hours. Rather, it runs parallel to our anxieties, becomes the repository of our fears. The darkness of the jungle approximates darkness everywhere, adumbrating the blackness of Conrad's humor, the despair of his irony. . . .

The problem of Marlow, as we saw earlier, is the problem of Conrad's art: to communicate the weight and depth of an experience which is uniquely felt. . . .

The story in fact has form: from the opening frame, with Marlow's somewhat ingenuous listeners, to the closing sequence, with Kurtz's innocent fiancée confirming her illusions. The use of a first-person narrative, through the agency of Marlow, was necessary so that Conrad could gain aesthetic distance and the reader could identify with an average man thrown into an abnormal situation. We must, Conrad realized, go through it with him and Marlow. Lacking the narrator, the story would appear too distant from the immediate experience—as though it had happened and was now over, like ancient history. From this safe distance, everyone was saved, and the evil force, Kurtz, rightfully had perished. But that is not at all Conrad's story; to make a morality play out of the tale is to destroy its felt sense. The story is concerned with hidden terrors in the normal heart, with the attractions of the unspeakable which we all experience, with the sense of power we wish to exert or identify with, ultimately with the underground existence each sentient being recognizes in himself. In this respect, Marlow as direct participant through his narration becomes indispensable.

So, too, in other respects did Conrad work out the shape of the story, in large and in details: through doubling of scenes and characters, through repetition, analogy, duplicating images, through difference of tone. From the beginning, when the ancient Romans on the Thames are contrasted with the modern Europeans on the Congo, Conrad used heightening and foreshortening, contrast and comparison to give the novella form. Most obviously, Marlow's peaceful setting on the *Nellie* is set off against his nightmarish Congo riverboat setting; in a different way, Kurtz's two fiancées, are contrasted, each one standing for certain values, indeed for entire cultures, in conflict; further, the jungle is set off against the river, with jungle as death, river as possible relief; in another way, Kurtz is compared with other forms of evil, with the deceptive smoothness of the station manager, with the hypocrisy of the pilgrims; the pilgrims in

turn are ironically compared with the savages they con-
demn, with the pilgrims less Christian than the pagan natives; within the natives, the tribal savages are contrasted
with those exposed to civilization, detribalized as it were, the
latter already full of wiles and deceit; light and dark, the
painter's chiaroscuro,[4] hover over the entire story, no less
important here than in Milton's Christian epic, *Paradise
Lost;* day dream and night dream form contrasts, worked out
in the play between expectation and consequence, between
professed ideals and realistic behavior, between Kurtz's humanitarianism and his barbarism, between Marlow's
middle-class sense of English justice and the Congo reality,
between the fluctuating love-and-hate which fill both Kurtz
and Marlow.

Out of the infinite possibilities facing Conrad, he chose
these to give unity to his language and ideas. Such devices
shape our thoughts and give form to our responses; they,
too, become the substance of our awareness. . . .

What makes this story so impressive is Conrad's ability to
focus on the Kurtz-Marlow polarity as a definition of our
times. European history as well as the history of individual
men can be read more clearly in the light of Conrad's art; for
he tells us that the most dutiful of men, a Marlow, can be led
to the brink of savagery and brutality if the will to power
touches him; that the most idealistic of men, Kurtz, can become a sadistic murderer; that the dirty work of this world
is carried out by men whose reputations are preserved by
lies. Conrad's moral tale becomes, in several respects, our
story, the only way we can read history and each other. [His-
torian] Hannah Arendt's definition of the "banality of evil,"
the nihilism of the average man, is fully relevant. It is a terrible story. Unlike Marlow, who possesses threads of heroism, we fail to confront it and prefer to acquiesce in our humiliation.

4. the arrangement of light and dark shading in a picture

CHAPTER 2

Kurtz and Marlow

READINGS ON
HEART OF DARKNESS

The Corruption of Kurtz

Robert F. Lee

Although Robert F. Lee acknowledges that Kurtz goes to the Congo with a purpose, he condemns what he becomes. In particular Lee cites two deplorable acts: Kurtz's ordering natives to fire on the steamer and his use of the African woman. He concludes that Kurtz is a moral failure. Robert F. Lee has taught at the College of Steubenville in Ohio. His interest lies in politics and imperialism in literature, topics about which he has written.

In *Heart of Darkness* Kurtz is . . . an ethical, material, and spiritual failure so foul, so abysmal, so depraved as to create awe, and thereby a false sense of magnificence. Kurtz is as intrinsically rotten as the putrid hippopotamus flesh the cannibals bring on board the river steamer commanded by Marlow. Out of "legitimate self-defence", because of its nauseous stench, a great amount of the hippopotamus flesh is thrown overboard. Conrad alludes to the meat later in the story in context more direct than in its first appearance. . . .

> The earth for us is a place to live in, where we must put up with sights, with sounds, with smells, too, by Jove! — breathe dead hippo, so to speak, and not be contaminated. And there, don't you see? your strength comes in, the faith in your ability for the digging of unostentatious holes to bury the stuff in — your power of devotion, not to yourself, but to an obscure, back-breaking business.

Kurtz' relation to the hippopotamus flesh is more apparent when we remember that the day after he died, "the pilgrims buried something in a muddy hole". . . .

THE COLONIAL IDEA, ITS IDEAL

Marlow, chatting with his cronies as they sit aboard a vessel moored in the Thames, contemplates the number of ships

Excerpted from *Conrad's Colonialism*, by Robert F. Lee (The Hague: Mouton, 1969). Reprinted by permission of Mouton de Gruyter, a division of Walter de Gruyter GmbH & Co., Berlin and New York.

which had in the past left that waterway "bearing the sword, and often the torch, messengers of the might within the land, bearers of a spark from the sacred fire". What follows is the depiction of the collapse of one man who, going out for the same reason as the "ships", but void of appreciation of the "idea", finally becomes governed by "a flabby, pretending, weak-eyed devil of a rapacious and pitiless folly". . . .

In the beginning, Kurtz has a sense of the "idea". When he first arrives in Africa he expresses the belief that "each station should be like a beacon on the road towards better things, a centre for trade of course, but also for humanizing, improving, instructing". The Belgian company's comment on this approach comes out of the manager, "Conceive you — that ass!" who then chokes with excessive indignation.

It was no unconscious act on Conrad's part that, having clearly differentiated between the Kurtz who first came to Africa and the abomination who died there, he relates the early Kurtz to his Anglo-Saxon heritage:

> The original Kurtz had been educated partly in England, and — as he was good enough to say himself — his sympathies were in the right place. His mother was half-English.

This very casual and unobtrusive device in Conrad's works repeatedly relates the good qualities of even bad characters to some English connections or influence.

Further evidence of his sympathies' being in the right place appears in his report Marlow discovers, which was to have been sent back to Europe for publication in the journal of the "International Society for the Suppression of Savage Customs". In magnificent language Kurtz expounds the argument that because of our developments we "must necessarily appear to them [savages] in the nature of supernatural beings — we approach them with the might as of a deity. . . . By the simple exercise of our will we can exert a power for good practically unbounded. . . ." However, Kurtz reveals a horrifying method as his final judgment for the solution of the Negro problem in a note scrawled much later at the foot of the last page: "Exterminate all the brutes!"

MARLOW FINDS IN KURTZ THE ANTITHESIS OF THE IDEA

In the light of Kurtz' early expressions of purpose and his reputation for ability about which Marlow had heard much, it is no wonder that Marlow had been most anxious, exceedingly anxious, to meet this man. What he met was the antithesis of what he expected. Kurtz' collapse with regard to his own stated ideas was towering. The "power for good" which he exerted consisted of raiding the countryside with the help of a tribe of savages whom he used as a tool and weapon. He substituted for trade goods the use of cartridges in obtaining the ends which developed after he gave up the high ideals of his report. "The wilderness", which is easily interpreted as the great challenge to Kurtz or any other man of intelligence or ambition, "had taken him, loved him, embraced him", and because he did not have it in him to see through to the "idea", "got into his veins, consumed his flesh, and sealed his soul to its own by the inconceivable ceremonies of some devilish initiation". His foul desires "caused him to preside at certain midnight dances ending with unspeakable rites, which — as far as I reluctantly gathered from what I heard at various times — were offered up to him". They also awakened "brutal instincts, by the memory of gratified and monstrous passions". His inability to meet the challenge "had driven him out to the edge of the forest, to the brush, towards the gleam of fires, the throb of drums, the drone of weird incantations; this alone had beguiled his unlawful soul beyond the bounds of permitted aspirations".

This depravity cannot be laid at the feet of the primitives who catered to him in his failure, for he was the "deity", he could have been the "power for good" if he had had the "will". His depravity does not stop with "gratified and monstrous passions". His egotistic selfishness was overwhelming. . . . "You should have heard him say, 'My ivory.' Oh yes, I heard him. 'My Intended, my ivory, my station, my river, my —' everything belonged to him." "I saw him open his mouth wide — it gave him a weirdly voracious aspect, as though he had wanted to swallow all the air, all the earth, all the men before him." The last phrase is not merely figurative when we remember Kurtz is in cannibal country.

And what, in the concrete, was that gaping maw devouring as a dainty, as a desire? Conrad gives us an example of the barbaric savagery for which the civilized Kurtz had failed — a Negress:

> She walked with measured steps, draped in striped and fringed cloths, treading the earth proudly, with a slight jingle and flash of barbarous ornaments. She carried her head high; her hair was done in the shape of a helmet; she had brass leg-

gings to the knee, brass wire gauntlets to the elbow, a crimson spot on her tawny cheek, innumerable necklaces of glass
beads on her neck; bizarre things, charms, gifts of witch-men,
that hung about her, glittered and trembled at every step.

This passage is stronger as a symbol of the shoddy when we
remember the care and delight Conrad takes in describing
the gold, jewels, and magnificent fabrics of the native
women in his Malay and other Eastern settings. Marlow
comments earlier in the story on the poor quality of the trade
"fringed-cloth". . . . Aïssa is beautiful whereas this Negress is
"savage and superb". Matara's sister counts the magnificent
pearls given her by the Dutchman; the Negress has "glass
beads" and "charms" (dried animal parts, more than likely)
given her by "witch-men". . . .

KURTZ FAILS BLACKS, EUROPEANS, EVERYONE

It has been shown how Kurtz failed the "blacks". He also
fails his own people. On the way up the river to investigate
what has happened to Kurtz, rumors of his illness having
reached the company's main station, the river steamer with
the Belgian officials and Marlow on board is attacked by
savages. Marlow is the man who makes the startling discovery "that it was Kurtz who had ordered the attack to be made
on the steamer". He ordered it with the idea of frightening
the steamer back, knowing, however, that possibly some
whites as well as many of his "tribe" would be killed. This
lack of concern is indirectly criticized, in that Marlow's
sense of responsibility for his native helmsman, "a savage
who was no more account than a grain of sand in a black
Sahara", is quite strongly stressed. "I had to look after him, I
worried about his deficiencies, and thus a subtle bond had
been created, of which I only became aware when it was
suddenly broken." This unconscious assumption bespeaks a
finer trait in Marlow than if all his care had been premeditated. "I missed my late helmsman awfully, — I missed him
even while his body was still lying in the pilot-house." Marlow had closed the shutter of the wheel house on the jungle
side, but the "poor fool" had opened it and been pierced by a
spear. Marlow tosses him overboard during the running battle, determined that the "very second-rate helmsman" would
be eaten by the fishes instead of the cannibals on the
steamer. They had been without their customary food for
some time.

In this tangle of degradation, the aspect most condemning Kurtz is his cosmic irresponsibility in not realizing how untrue all of the "mine" is. "Everything belonged to him — but that was a trifle. The thing was to know what he belonged to. . . ." No matter how awful was Kurtz' lack of intrinsic worth, there was not even diabolical dignity, since he was completely cut loose from any ideal or any principle. This in itself created a dangerous problem, for when Kurtz "escaped" from the river-boat and returned to the village, endangering the ship and all on board, Marlow, attempting to bring him back, was faced with the situation of dealing with a man to whom he "could not appeal in the name of anything high or low".

> If he makes a row we are lost, I thought to myself. This clearly was not a case for fisticuffs, even apart from the very natural aversion I had to beat that Shadow — this wandering and tormented thing. "You will be lost", I said — "utterly lost". One gets sometimes such a flash of inspiration, you know. I did say the right thing, though indeed he could not have been more irretrievably lost than he was at this very moment. . . .
> "I had immense plans", he muttered irresolutely. . . . "I was on the threshold of great things", he pleaded, in a voice of longing, with a wistfulness of tone that made my blood run cold.

It is no compliment to us that Kurtz could be told, "Your success in Europe is assured in any case", that he could succeed in our civilization but not where he must be governed by the "idea". In the final analysis, his entire collapse is due to his being "hollow at the core", without identity.

Marlow was unable to tell Kurtz' Intended his last words since "it would have been too dark — too dark altogether". Expecting the heavens to fall on his head, he informs the young lady that Kurtz' last syllables were her name, instead of, as we know, an unconscious realization of himself — "the horror! the horror!"

Kurtz as the Incarnation of Evil

R.A. Gekoski

> R.A. Gekoski's analysis concludes that Kurtz is the incarnation of evil. Gekoski contends that Kurtz starts out being idealistic in his aims. But once he is allowed complete freedom to order his universe, he uses it for evil aims to become a devil rather than a savior. R.A. Gekoski attended Oxford University, where he studied literature and wrote his doctoral thesis on Joseph Conrad.

In 'Heart of Darkness', Conrad takes his deepest look into the human condition, and comes to perhaps his most pessimistic conclusions on the various and incompatible pressures that can be imposed on the human spirit. . . . We cannot, in fact, adequately understand 'Heart of Darkness' if we do not begin by considering in structural terms the relationship that it establishes between Kurtz and Marlow. . . . Indeed, Kurtz's crucial role in the tale lies in his symbolic importance: in the representative quality of his history, in his role as a final incarnation of the darkness itself, and as a potential aspect of Marlow's own self. . . .

KURTZ'S APPETITE AND HUNGER

Chapter 3 begins with Marlow's encounter with Kurtz's Russian disciple—an incident of some importance in delaying, and setting the tone for, Marlow's approaching meeting with Kurtz. The Russian sees Kurtz as a noble soul, entitled by his innate qualities to the magisterial enactment of his own desires. This view—balancing that of Kurtz as a merely lawless ivory hunter—places him (in [German philosopher Friedrich] Nietzsche's phrase) 'beyond good and evil'—'You can't judge Mr Kurtz as you would an ordinary man'—and implicitly poses one of the story's major questions: how *is* Kurtz to be judged? The desire to answer this question underlies Marlow's anticipation of the much delayed meeting with Kurtz, who has just returned from a long journey with another gigantic lot of ivory. This 'appetite for more ivory', which we have seen to be linked to a less easily satisfied spiritual hunger, is soon associated with the colour of the skeleton heads with which Kurtz adorns his house. Marlow is not so much shocked by the sight of the heads, as by what they reveal about the state of mind of Mr Kurtz:

> 'They only showed that Mr Kurtz lacked restraint in the gratification of his various lusts, that there was something wanting in him—some small matter which, when the pressing need arose, could not be found under his magnificent eloquence. Whether he knew of this deficiency himself I can't say. I think the knowledge came to him at last—only at the very last. But the wilderness had found him out early, and had taken on him a terrible vengeance for the fantastic invasion. I think it had whispered to him things about himself which he did not know, things of which he had no conception till he took counsel with this great solitude—and the whisper had proved irresistibly fascinating. It echoed loudly within him because he was hollow at the core . . .'

The symbolic association of the ivory with the heads outside Kurtz's house is then extended until it suggests the very essence of Kurtz himself; Marlow's first description of the man neatly combines the two images:

> 'I could see the cage of his ribs all astir, the bones of his arm waving. It was as though an animated image of death carved out of old ivory had been shaking its hand with menaces at a motionless crowd of men made of dark and glittering bronze. I saw him open his mouth wide—it gave him a weirdly voracious aspect, as though he had wanted to swallow all the air, all the earth, all the men before him.'

But we are never to know the secret of Mr Kurtz's degradation, nor the nature of the 'abominable satisfactions' in which he has immersed himself. This is only mildly frustrating, certainly not an artistic failure. Nothing is so uninteresting . . . as a detailed description of abominable satisfactions.

MARLOW'S IDENTIFICATION WITH KURTZ

The Manager of the Central Station, impressed yet disturbed by the huge amounts of ivory that Kurtz has collected, expresses to Marlow the opinion that the ivory trade will be ruined by Kurtz's 'unsound method'. This phrase, glibly bypassing all of the unspeakable evils which Kurtz has perpetrated, appals Marlow. It is at this point that his identification with

Kurtz first becomes explicit, for in his assertion that Kurtz is nevertheless 'a remarkable man' he chooses to side with him against the Manager and his fellow 'fools'. The decision is embodied in the phrase 'a choice of nightmares', by which Marlow attempts to justify his sympathy with the full-blooded egoism of Kurtz rather than with the nasty equivocation of the 'pilgrims' and their like. But really he is responding not so much to Kurtz as to what Kurtz may be said to represent:

'I had turned to the wilderness really, not to Mr Kurtz, who, I was ready to admit, was as good as buried. And for a moment it seemed to me as if I also were buried in a vast grave full of unspeakable secrets. I felt an intolerable weight oppressing my breast, the smell of the damp earth, the unseen presence of victorious corruption, the darkness of an impenetrable night . . .'

The threat that Kurtz represents becomes increasingly real to Marlow as his knowledge of the man (and, by extension, of himself), and his distance from the saving grace of everyday work, increase. He recognizes that only he can seek Kurtz out after his remarkable escape:

'I did not betray Mr Kurtz—it was ordered I should never betray him—it was written I should be loyal to the nightmare of my choice. I was anxious to deal with this shadow by myself alone,—and to this day I don't know why I was so jealous of sharing with anyone the peculiar blackness of that experience.'

Like that of James Wait at the end of *The Nigger of the 'Narcissus'*, Kurtz's role is now almost purely symbolic: he, too, is a 'blackness' that must somehow be resisted.

As Marlow blindly searches the jungles, recognizing (perhaps a bit conveniently) that he is confusing the beating of drums with that of his heart, he comes upon an ill and desperate Kurtz crawling back towards the savage enclave of which he is the adored leader. This ultimate struggle of will between Marlow and Kurtz can easily be misunderstood. [Critic and biographer] Jocelyn Baines, for instance, asserts that Marlow 'is even able to wrest Kurtz from the grasp of the wilderness when he is drawn back to it', which greatly oversimplifies the scene. Marlow does make the statement ('You will be lost . . . utterly lost') that sways Kurtz in his tortured conflict, but it is Kurtz alone who finally resists the virtually irresistible call of the darkness, and allows himself to be led back to 'civilization'. Had he chosen to 'make a row', Kurtz would have been heard, and rescued, by the natives. But he does not do so, and this is perhaps the basis of his final triumph, and of Marlow's fidelity to his memory.

In his description of their struggle, Marlow gives us the key to the puzzling and terrifying character of Kurtz:

'I had to deal with a being to whom I could not appeal in the name of anything high or low. I had, even like the niggers, to invoke him—himself—his own exalted and incredible degradation. There was nothing either above or below him, and I knew it. He had kicked himself loose of the earth. Confound the man! he had kicked the very earth to pieces. He was alone, and I before him did not know whether I stood on the ground or floated in the air. I've been telling you what we said—repeating the phrases we pronounced—but what's the good? They were common everyday words—the familiar, vague sounds exchanged on every waking day of life. But what of that? They had behind them, to my mind, the terrific suggestiveness of words heard in dreams, of phrases spoken in nightmares. Soul! If anybody has ever struggled with a soul, I am the man. And I wasn't arguing with a lunatic either. Believe me or not, his intelligence was perfectly clear—concentrated, it is true, upon himself with horrible intensity, yet clear; and therein was my only chance—barring of course, the killing him there and then, which wasn't so good, on account of the unavoidable noise. But his soul was mad. Being alone in the wilderness, it had looked within itself, and, by heavens! I tell you, it had gone mad. I had—for my sins, I suppose—to go through the ordeal of looking into it myself. No eloquence could have been so withering to one's belief in mankind as his final burst of sincerity. He struggled with himself, too. I saw it, —I heard it. I saw the inconceivable mystery of a soul that knew no restraint, no faith, and no fear, yet struggling blindly with itself.'

Several phrases early in the passage—'a being to whom I could not appeal in the name of anything high or low', 'There was nothing either above or below him', 'He had kicked himself loose from the earth', and, particularly, 'He was alone'—suggest that Kurtz cannot be taken simply as a symbol of transcendental evil; it is now clear that Kurtz's fate is of general interest because it is a consequence of his isolation, of his absolute freedom. He is a fully autonomous man, attempting to generate and enact his own moral truths, confronting the results of his freedom. In this passage we find the germinal 'idea' of the story (to which Conrad had referred in his letter to Cunninghame Graham) most clearly embodied: that 'safety' and 'value' are illusions that can only be generated and preserved within a given society, while any attempt to place oneself outside these artificial, but necessary, moral structures will drive any *man* into a perilous condition of 'excited imagination'. The Manager of the Central Station and the other 'fools' of the story can never descend to the 'heart of darkness' because they have no 'imagination'. What makes Kurtz remarkable is not only that he has lived in the darkness, but also chosen to leave it. *It* never leaves him, nor any man who has confronted it. We are never told the grounds on which Kurtz makes his final choice, and we may perhaps be left wondering why it is that Kurtz, who had been described as 'hollow at the core', could suddenly become capable of his final, remarkable, victory.

KURTZ'S IDEALISM TWISTED INTO EGOISM

It seems there are different kinds of hollowness, differently resonant. The Manager and brickmaker are simply void; Kurtz's hollowness contains the nothingness of his universe. Like [novelist] E.M. Forster's Marabar Caves, Kurtz echoes the final meaninglessness of all things.

That Kurtz's soul should become the theatre in which this 'boum' echoes is not because he is immoral, but the reverse: he is the prototype of the idealistic man. His pamphlet (written for the International Society for the Suppression of Savage Customs) is charged with naïve eloquence about the role of the white man in raising the natives to a 'civilized' state, and presents what is at first glance an appealing moral position, faintly similar to [short-story writer Rudyard] Kipling:

> 'He began with the argument that we whites, from the point of development we had arrived at, "must necessarily appear to them (savages) in the nature of supernatural beings—we approach them with the might as of a deity", and so on, and so on. "By the simple exercise of our will we can exert a power for good practically unbounded," etc., etc.'

By taking advantage of conditions which allow him to assume the role of the benevolent deity, the white man can exercise his unlimited power towards good—or any other end that he chooses. Yet the assumption that a man in a state of absolute freedom will do good is nonsense; at the very 'heart of darkness' every man desires, like Kurtz, to 'take a high seat among the devils of the land.' Hence we have Kurtz's final scrawl at the bottom of his pamphlet, 'Exterminate all the brutes!' Kurtz's fate is that of any man who attempts to take upon himself the entire structure of morality. . . .

MARLOW'S INTERPRETATION OF KURTZ'S "HORROR!"

When Kurtz dies on the steamer taking him down the Congo, his last words, 'The horror! The horror!', impressive and even terrifying as they are, are nevertheless thoroughly ambiguous. They might represent Kurtz's final desire to return to the scene of those abominable satisfactions, be his judgment on the unworthiness of his end, a comment on the human condition, or a vision of eternal damnation. Marlow, however, is certain of his own interpretation; he sees Kurtz's last words as a confession, as a final attempt at self-purification: 'a judgment upon the adventures of his soul upon this earth':

> 'This is the reason why I affirm that Kurtz was a remarkable man. He had something to say. He said it. Since I had peeped over the edge myself, I understand better the meaning of his stare, that could not see the flame of the candle, but was wide enough to embrace the whole universe, piercing enough to penetrate all the hearts that beat in the darkness. He had summed up—he had judged. "The horror!"'

At the 'heart of darkness', it seems, there is a piercing clarity—a vision of man's fate so unendurable that it can only remain nameless:

> 'He was a remarkable man. After all, this was the expression of some sort of belief; it had candour, it had conviction, it had a vibrating note of revolt in its whisper, it had the appalling face of a glimpsed truth—the strange commingling of desire and hate . . . It is his extremity that I seem to have lived through. True, he had made that last stride, he had stepped over the edge, while I had been permitted to draw back my hesitating foot. And perhaps in this is the whole difference; perhaps all the wisdom, and all truth, and all sincerity, are just compressed into that inappreciable moment of time in which we step over the threshold of the invisible. Perhaps! I like to think my summing-up would not have been a word of careless contempt. Better his cry—much better. It was an affirmation, a moral victory paid for by innumerable defeats, by abominable terrors, by abominable satisfactions. But it was a victory! That is why I have remained loyal to Kurtz to the last . . .'

Kurtz's final vision, then, is one both of the human predicament and of his own experience—is both general and particular, as [critic] J.I.M. Stewart points out:

> 'Kurtz's evil courses—and this is the final terror of the fable —have brought him to the heart of an impenetrable darkness in which it is yet possible to *see* more than can be seen in daylight by those to whom no such journey had befallen. Kurtz's last words are a statement of the widest generality. They define one tenable view of man's situation in an alien universe. Alternatively, they define the only sense of himself that man can bring back from a wholly inward journey: that into the immense darkness, the unmeaning anarchy, of his own psyche.'

In the light of this interpretation of Kurtz's final words, then, it seems that we must go back and re-evaluate exactly what Marlow meant when he indicted Kurtz as 'hollow at the core'. If Kurtz's fate is, as it seems, of universal significance, then to what extent can his degradation be said to be due to his inner hollowness? Marlow's remark that Kurtz's final words were an affirmation and a victory seems to contradict an earlier assertion that Kurtz was 'hollow at the core'. We appear to have two conflicting strands operating in 'Heart of Darkness': one which makes a distinction between those men who are 'hollow' and those who have 'inborn strength', while the other seems to regard Kurtz as a remarkable man who has made a journey into the self which few men could have endured. We may perhaps be left with the thought that the judgments that one makes about autonomous individuals are very different from the judgments that one makes about individuals as they relate to some social organization. Kurtz's egoism may damn him, but he is a remarkable man. Again, we turn to Nietzsche for a key to the enigma of Kurtz:

> 'Something might be true although at the same time harmful and dangerous in the highest degree; indeed, it could pertain to the fundamental nature of existence that a complete knowledge of it would destroy one—so that the strength of a spirit could be measured by how much "truth" it could take, more clearly, to what degree it *needed* it attenuated, veiled, sweetened, blunted, and falsified.'

Kurtz—like his successor, Martin Decoud of *Nostromo*—sees too much, too clearly, to live through the experience.

Marlow's Evolving Awareness

Lawrence Graver

Lawrence Graver analyzes Marlow in terms of his Congo trip, including his worldview before the trip, what he learns on it, and the changes in his outlook after he emerges from the jungle. Graver particularly focuses on Marlow's reaction to the ivory trade and his fascination with Kurtz. Lawrence Graver has taught English at the University of California in Los Angeles and at Williams College in Williamstown, Massachusetts. He is the author of *Carson McCullers, Samuel Beckett: The Critical Heritage*, and *Mastering the Film*.

Recent criticism has made readers look more attentively at the way in which the frame of "Heart of Darkness" is pieced together. Since the progress of Marlow is the main subject of the story, the importance of "presentation" as such is obvious, and "Heart of Darkness" is only partially understood if one fails to consider its remarkable narrative mode. However, there are other problems about the handling of theme and character in the story that have to be approached in a more old-fashioned way. Although the difference between showing and telling can explain certain things about Conrad's art, a more traditional question can be just as helpful in coming to an understanding of this difficult story: What kind of man was Marlow before, during, and after the Congo experience?

In "Youth," forty-two-year-old Marlow reminisces about himself at twenty; in "Heart of Darkness" the subject for contemplation is now closer to thirty, and the passage of nearly a decade has made all the difference. In the first story, the older man contrasts naïveté and experience; in the second, he describes the critical moment when the innocent went stumbling across the shadow line. We first glimpse the older Marlow on

Excerpted from *Conrad's Short Fiction*, by Lawrence Graver (Berkeley and Los Angeles: University of California Press). Copyright © 1969 The Regents of the University of California. Reprinted by permission of the publisher.

deck of the *Nellie,* where he sits in his familiar pose of gloomy meditation. His portentous opening, "and this also has been one of the dark places of the earth," is followed by a warning from the anonymous narrator that the pallid figure about to speak does not resemble the ordinary seaman. Unlike most sailors, who are as a rule sedentary and unreflective, Marlow is a wanderer with a long history of cheerless introspection, who now tells stories of a vaguely evocative kind. When Marlow resumes the narration, his skeptical remarks about history and heroism reveal not only his contemplative nature and the range of his reading but his complex understanding of the relationship between past and present. The main point of his opening comments on Roman Britain—the difference between an informed and an uninformed egoism—is one that only a man of some experience can recognize. Thus, despite his melancholy, Marlow is accepted immediately as an authoritative guide to the events that follow; later he will emerge as the spokesman for the positive values of the story.

VANITY AND GREED JAR MARLOW'S NAÏVE CONFIDENCE

The important fact about Marlow's dark wisdom is that it hardly existed before the trip to the Congo. The young man who saw a map of Africa in a London shop front and decided to follow his childhood dream is, at the start, an instinctive egoist, motivated by little more than an impatient desire for adventure. At first, he moves briskly through the company offices in Brussels, his exuberance checked only by a slowly developing suspicion of the lunacy of his employers. This suspicion, awakened by an encounter with the startling grotesques who staff the company offices, remains mild for the moment. Despite the two knitting phantoms, the witch-like secretary "full of desolation and sympathy," the clerk who quotes [Greek philosopher] Plato while hinting at cabalistic knowledge,[1] and the maniacal doctor who painstakingly measures the heads of the damned, Marlow leaves the building uneasy but still confident. In a final interview with his aunt, he good-naturedly jests at her solicitude and naïveté, and manfully boasts of his own sensitivity to the economic foundations of reality.

Once the African journey gets under way, however, disquietude quickly replaces confidence as Marlow is instructed in the absurdity of his situation. Shocked by knowledge of wide-

---

1. acquired by mysterious art; understood by a specially initiated small group

spread mismanagement and folly, he forsakes the mild jokes about the profit motive and turns to desperate irony at the criminality of these "high and just proceedings." From the day he left Europe until he had reached the outer station along the Congo River, Marlow's sense of Africa had been negative but abstract; for he never stopped long enough to get a particular-

MARLOW'S EVOLVING AWARENESS

In the dark night of the jungle near dancing natives and ceremonial fires, Marlow finds Kurtz crawling on all fours, as if the wilderness had cast a spell over him.

As soon as I got on the bank I saw a trail—a broad trail through the grass. I remember the exaltation with which I said to myself, 'He can't walk—he is crawling on all-fours—I've got him.' The grass was wet with dew. I strode rapidly with clenched fists. . . .

I came upon him, and, if he had not heard me coming, I would have fallen over him, too, but he got up in time. He rose, unsteady, long, pale, indistinct, like a vapour exhaled by the earth, and swayed slightly, misty and silent before me; while at my back the fires loomed between the trees, and the murmur of many voices issued from the forest. . . .

Though he could hardly stand, there was still plenty of vigour in his voice. 'Go away—hide yourself,' he said, in that profound tone. It was very awful. I glanced back. We were within thirty yards from the nearest fire. A black figure stood up, strode on long black legs, waving long black arms, across the glow. It had horns—antelope horns, I think—on its head. Some sorcerer, some witch-man, no doubt; it looked fiendlike enough. 'Do you know what you are doing?' I whispered. 'Perfectly,' he answered, raising his voice for that single word: it sounded to me far off and yet loud, like a hail through a speaking-trumpet. . . .

'I was on the threshold of great things,' he pleaded, in a voice of longing, with a wistfulness of tone that made my blood run cold. . . .

I tried to break the spell—the heavy, mute spell of the wilderness—that seemed to draw him to its pitiless breast by the awakening of forgotten and brutal instincts, by the memory of gratified and monstrous passions. This alone, I was convinced, had driven him out to the edge of the forest, to the bush, towards the gleam of fires, the throb of drums, the drone of weird incantations; this alone had beguiled his unlawful soul beyond the bounds of permitted aspirations.

Joseph Conrad, *Heart of Darkness.*

ized impression. Now, however, at the first station, he learns something concrete about man's role in the squalid drama of exploitation. His first teacher is the company's chief accountant, a man so devoted to correct ledger entries and to keeping up appearances that he is a lesson in the fortitude of ignorance and a living proof that vacuousness can have its wondrous side. In a landscape so dismal and a moral climate so corrupt, the accountant at least puts up a show; and Marlow reluctantly confesses that this mannikin earns a certain measure of amused respect, for his starched collars and elegant shirtfronts were unquestionably "achievements of character." Although stuffed with sawdust, the accountant and people like him nevertheless provide factitious support for the entire European effort in the Congo. It begins to dawn on Marlow that one source of power for an imperial operation comes from a direct and simple-minded vanity.

The other, more compulsive source of energy behind the African experiment is pure greed, a human quality about which Marlow learns a great deal in the Congo. Most of the officials who work at the various outposts of progress are, like the members of the Eldorado Exploring Expedition, "reckless without hardihood, greedy without audacity, and cruel without courage." Once in their midst, Marlow is forced to abandon his earlier notions about how money works in society. In a previous conversation with his aunt, when he had "ventured to hint that the company was run for profit," he assumed an air of tolerant superiority. Now, he realizes how shallow and inadequate his earlier ideas had been; for not only is the company "run for a profit," it is run, without the slightest decency, for profit without limit; and the men who run it emerge not as simple businessmen but as predatory adventurers, as "sordid buccaneers."

MARLOW LEARNS ABOUT THE JUNGLE, IMPERIALISM, AND KURTZ

Although Marlow's indictment mounts with impressive force throughout the story, it is finally a secondary element in Conrad's overall conception. As is perfectly obvious, the main burden of meaning and interest in "Heart of Darkness" is carried by Kurtz and Marlow, who in some fatal and obscure way are meant for one another. When Marlow first came to the coast of Africa, he had been a natural egoist who desired only to prove himself in an arduous situation. Although his intelligence and good nature were not nearly so obvious as his high spirits, he was undeniably quick witted, compassionate, and hard to fool. Once he begins to sail up the river, he learns his lesson immediately, recognizing that the jungle is a force of darkly ambiguous appeal and that the European enterprise—supported by fools and fortune hunters—is a criminal fiasco of the most scandalous kind.

No wonder, then, that he should respond favorably to the promise of meeting Kurtz. Conrad's teasing introduction of his demonic hero is justly famous: After an abrupt series of brief but tantalizing remarks, Marlow is ready to swear eternal loyalty to a man he has never seen. One close look at the portrait of Kurtz that emerges from these scraps of information will reveal why Marlow is so quickly seduced. In addition to his more obvious gifts of intelligence and creativity, Kurtz has two qualities that would immediately attract the younger man. Not only is he self-reliant and self-absorbed; he is a romantic idealist with a grandiose mission, "an emissary of pity, and science, and progress and devil knows what else." To Marlow's mind, Kurtz is his superior both in courage and in noble idealism, the two virtues that he himself values most highly.

In the days before his arrival at the inner station, Marlow thinks of Kurtz in two ways, first as the figure in a startling visual tableau and then as a disembodied voice, the tableau an emblem of Kurtz's natural egoism and the voice representative of his seemingly articulate idealism:

> As to me, I seemed to see Kurtz for the first time. It was a distinct glimpse: the dugout, four paddling savages, and the lone white man turning his back suddenly on the headquarters, on relief, on thoughts of home—perhaps; setting his face towards the depths of the wilderness, towards his empty and desolate station. I did not know the motive. Perhaps he was just simply a fine fellow who stuck to his work for its own sake.

> The man presented himself as a voice. Not of course that I did not connect him with some sort of action. Hadn't I been told in all the tones of jealousy and admiration that he had collected, bartered, swindled, or stolen more ivory than all the other agents together? That was not the point. The point was in his being a gifted creature, and that of all his gifts the one that stood out preeminently, that carried with it a sense of real presence, was his ability to talk, his words—the gift of expression, the bewildering, the illuminating, the most exalted and the most contemptible, the pulsating stream of light, or the deceitful flow from the heart of an impenetrable darkness.

MARLOW ATTRACTED TO KURTZ

Marlow's initial response to Kurtz is based, then, on the two most obvious qualities in his own makeup. Yet each time he discovers something new about his nemesis, his allegiance becomes that much more paradoxical. Admittedly, Conrad's presentation of Kurtz is not notable for its clarity, and a reader is never quite sure how much of the mystery surrounding him is the product of art and how much of evasion. Nevertheless, the source of Kurtz's spectacular appeal can be traced back to his obsessive egoism. Although Marlow never denies that Kurtz's moral idealism has become moral barbarism, that his admirable self-sufficiency has degenerated into an overwhelming pride in "my Intended, my station, my career, my ideas," he insists that Kurtz is remarkable for having the true courage of his hallucination: "He won't be forgotten. Whatever he was, he was not common. He had the power to charm or frighten rudimentary souls into an aggravated witch-dance in his honour; he could also fill the small souls of the pilgrims with bitter misgivings: he had one devoted friend at least; and he had conquered one soul in the world that was neither rudimentary nor tainted with self-seeking."

This passage offers an important clue to the riddle of Kurtz's charismatic attraction. In a world filled with rudimentary and greedy egoists, Kurtz—despite his charlatanism—at least has the imagination to conceive of greatness and the single-mindedness to carry his dream to its inevitable, terrifying conclusion. On one hand, he can write an eloquent report that appeals to "every altruistic sentiment" and, on the other, is demoniacal enough to end it with the postscript, "exterminate all the brutes." One day he will seem, in a "weirdly voracious aspect," to "swallow all the air, all the earth, all the men before him," but on another will accept the implications of his moral extravagance and judge life as "the horror, the horror."

In one respect, Kurtz resembles a familiar type in the literature of the past two hundred years—the presumptive outlaw who gains a degree of admiration by crossing the boundaries of conventional morality and exploring the possibilities of living on the other side. But this is not the final image that Conrad wishes us to take away from the story. Kurtz is less an inspiration than a warning. For all its audacity, his life is a chilling demonstration of the destructive extremities of pure ego and the price one pays for trying to live outside civilization: "I had to deal with a being to whom I could not appeal in the name of anything high or low. I had, even like the niggers, to invoke him—himself—his own exalted and incredible degradation. There was nothing either above or below him, and I knew it. He had kicked himself loose of the earth." This total isolation comes to Kurtz only after he has passed through nearly all the familiar stages of Conradian egoism. Starting as a venturesome natural egoist, he talks himself into an obsessive concern with civilizing the natives, becomes torn by his desire for wealth and power, and is finally driven to sequester himself as the most voracious divinity of the land. As such, Kurtz is the first of Conrad's characters to embody nearly all the egoistical compulsions that keep reappearing in the novels and stories, and to attach them to an idea which, in conception at least, appears to be altruistic. Although Kurtz's initial idealism is eventually shown to have been shallow all along, he never quite loses his fatal charisma; and despite Marlow's recognition that the "gorgeous eloquence" was without substance, Kurtz can never be wholly repudiated.

Kurtz—A Representational Character, A Symbol

Much of Kurtz's forcefulness comes from his representative nature, for Conrad uses him to say as much as he could at this point in his life about the claims and consequences of human egoism. It is also this exemplary quality that makes Kurtz so shadowy as a human being. As a rule, when Conrad describes an obsessive or a sequestered egoist, he sacrifices the verisimilitude of conventional character portrayal and concentrates on making the man a convincing emblem of some broad pattern of human conduct. Many of the details about Kurtz describe his actions in an obviously symbolic way and are more closely related to the meaning of his Satanic quest than to his specific characteristics as a human being. After reading "Heart of Darkness" one is more apt to remember the savage decline and fall of European idealism than the fate of a particular individual. Even such exceptionally vivid concrete details as Kurtz's luminous bald head and his fantastically long body seem chosen to make an ironical larger point; the baldness of his head corresponds to the ivory he so crassly covets, while his height belies the

Germanic origins of his name. Then, too, Kurtz is disembodied for another reason. Since one of the major themes of
"Heart of Darkness" is the hollowness and yet the enchanting
power of public rhetoric, Conrad presents Kurtz more often
"draped nobly in the folds of a gorgeous eloquence" than in
the traditional garments of an ordinary human being.

But whether Kurtz is emblem or individual, he has a decisive impact on Marlow's life. No one would argue anymore
that Marlow's education rather than Kurtz's adventure is the
center of interest in Conrad's story. Having begun as a self-
confident young adventurer, Marlow is painstakingly instructed in different kinds of evil, banal and otherwise,
learns things about himself that he hardly suspected, and
comes home in a state of complete shock. Yet despite the
psychic scars and the blasted imagination, Marlow does
emerge as wise in the lessons of complex altruism; and
since these are the most positive values in Conrad's universe, they require extended definition.

MARLOW'S CHARACTER PROTECTS HIM AND
LEADS HIM TO CHOOSE CIVILIZATION

The delicate balance between sympathy and revulsion in
Marlow's response to Kurtz—his ability to see him as both
an inspiration and a warning—is the product of a view of life
notable for its intelligence. Marlow's refusal to follow Kurtz
to the last stages of his dark exploration is based not so
much on the conventional man's cowardice as on his refined
sense of human paradox. The experience that Marlow un-
dergoes in the Congo is marked by an almost unbearable dou-
bleness: every vice has its seductive virtue; every virtue its
unsuspected, heartbreaking vice. Yet despite Marlow's attraction for Kurtz's peculiar kind of blackness, he finally accepts,
however cautiously, the price to be paid for civilization. This
acceptance is hard won and not without its own high cost.
Just as all Europe contributed to the making of Kurtz, so in
another sense did it contribute to the making of Marlow, the
man who comes to the wilderness protected by certain defenses against the darkness. These defenses—courage, loyalty, and pragmatism—are tested and shown to be artificial
props against a force that is clearly more natural. But Marlow accepts them as necessary and certainly preferable to no
defenses at all. They are preferable because his commitment
to civilization—to the past, present, and future of the race—

proves to be stronger than his commitment to certain forms of the truth. His lie to Kurtz's fiancée is in this sense an admission that civilization (and particularly simple altruists) must be protected from the truth about itself. Not always, but occasionally; for the fact that Marlow tells an accurate version of the story to the four men on the *Nellie* suggests that there are moments when the truth can be told.

The ultimate vision of the complex altruist is undeniably austere. Admitting the attraction of diabolism, he must nevertheless, from a sense of balance and continuity, reject extremes of human behavior; and yet by so doing he denies the possibility of those forms of heroism achieved only by the romantic egoist. Theatrical self-assertion, unchecked individualism, obsessive egoism—these are the paths to glory and self-destruction in a typical Conrad story. With his skeptical self-awareness and rejection of fanaticism, Marlow seems pale and anonymous in comparison with Kurtz. His survival leaves him with very little to cheer about.

"Heart of Darkness," then, is the second work in which Conrad treats the theme of egoism and altruism in a complex and memorable way. In *The Nigger of the "Narcissus"* the crew represents the full spectrum of egoistical possibility, while Captain Allistoun and to a lesser extent Mr. Baker speak for mature altruism. In the later work, Kurtz's hallucinatory egoism is in itself a composite of nearly all the patterns usually found in Conrad's work, while the pragmatic wisdom of Marlow provides the antithetical principles needed to make the dualism work. The melancholy affirmation of *The Nigger* becomes even harsher and more problematical in "Heart of Darkness." The essential conflict, however, is the same.

Marlow's Character Is Suited to His Task

Michael P. Jones

Michael P. Jones predicates his discussion of Marlow's character on the premise that an ultimate truth about life and death exists, but, because humans cannot know it and survive, they create a society of "lies," contrivances to shield them from the unknowable. Jones contends that Marlow discovers this truth and that he is a man of courage, intelligence, wisdom, and, finally, humanity. Jones wrote his doctoral thesis on Joseph Conrad while at Boston College.

In the beginning of "Heart of Darkness," there are several important developments in Conrad's imagination of the heroic ordeal. The first is that he isolates a knowledgeable, self-conscious narrator among an audience within the modern world and defines his moral perspectives according to both. The second is that he becomes explicitly concerned with the journey as a metaphysical and a verbal strategy—as a way to recover truth and to give some rhetorical shape to the process of discovering it. The third development is that he makes it the stated purpose of his journey to pursue a moral and ontological[1] inquiry into human history, and simultaneously into the human mind, that takes him back to a condition that precedes that of the fallen world. In "Heart of Darkness" there is no sense of a prelapsarian[2] paradise. There is no presumption of a Wordsworthian state of innocence.[3] "Heart of Darkness" does return us to the kind of Wordsworthian universe we have glimpsed in Book VI of *The Prelude* and Book I of *The Recluse*, but here the intimations of divinity are replaced by the shadows of a demonic darkness. . . .

1. concerned with the nature of being 2. pertaining to the period before the fall of Adam and Eve 3. a childlike innocence defined by Romantic poet William Wordsworth

Excerpted from Michael P. Jones, *Conrad's Heroism: A Paradise Lost* (Ann Arbor, MI: UMI Research Press, 1985). Copyright 1985 by Michael P. Jones. Reprinted by permission of the author.

Marlow's Role as Storyteller
and Searcher on Conrad's Journey

The focus of all these developments is one of the most remarkable characters of modern fiction, Marlow. The voice of
the first narrator serves largely to introduce Marlow and to
direct our attention to him as a narrator. It is a voice that is
distinct from that of Marlow, one that will virtually disap-
pear as Marlow begins to talk. . . .

Marlow's role as a storyteller is presented among the first
of his ambivalent perspectives, as he seems to be an interme-
diary between what is familiar and comprehensible and what
is obscure or unknown. "The yarns of seamen have a direct
simplicity," the first narrator says, "the whole meaning of
which lies within the shell of a cracked nut. But Marlow was
not typical (if his propensity to spin yarns is excepted), and to
him the meaning of an episode was not inside like a kernel
but outside, enveloping the tale which brought it out only as a
glow brings out a haze, in the likeness of one of these misty
halos that sometimes are made visible by the spectral illumi-
nation of moonshine." Just as Wordsworth did a century earlier in *The Recluse*, Conrad claims that the journey Marlow
makes and the story he tells will add a new dimension to our
conception of heroism. . . .

"Heart of Darkness" becomes the central tale among Conrad's adventure stories, for it represents the farthest extension
of his heroic journeys into the regions of the unknown. It
marks the end of the tradition of adventure tales . . . and the
failure of Conrad's romantic search for a universal truth. . . .

In "Heart of Darkness" Conrad begins with the idea of the
heroic journey and ends by scurrying back in terror to a civilization he views as both a refuge for the cowardly and a
demesne[4] of lunatics. Because the idea of heroism must un-
dergo several transformations during the course of this story, it
is necessary to define more exactly the heroism displayed by
Marlow as he enters and then emerges from the wilderness
and to discuss its relationship to Conrad's imagination of man.

Marlow's Qualities Fit Him for the Journey

In a traditional sense, certainly, Marlow is no coward. He is
clever, industrious, inventive; he is cool under the pressures of

---

4. a realm; a domain

A FLASHBACK OF KURTZ AND THE WILDERNESS

*As Marlow enters the home of Kurtz's Intended, a vision
flashes into his mind, scenes vivid with the sights, sounds,
and darkness of Kurtz and the wilderness. Just as this truth is
most immediate, Marlow rejects it and tells the Intended a lie.*

I thought his memory was like the other memories of the dead
that accumulate in every man's life—a vague impress on the
brain of shadows that had fallen on it in their swift and final
passage; but before the high and ponderous door, between the
tall houses of a street as still and decorous as a well-kept alley in
a cemetery, I had a vision of him on the stretcher, opening his
mouth voraciously, as if to devour all the earth with all its mankind. He lived then before me; he lived as much as he had ever
lived—a shadow insatiable of splendid appearances, of frightful
realities; a shadow darker than the shadow of the night, and
draped nobly in the folds of gorgeous eloquence. The vision
seemed to enter the house with me—the stretcher, the
phantom-bearers, the wild crowd of obedient worshippers, the
gloom of the forests, the glitter of the reach between the murky
bends, the beat of the drum, regular and muffled like the beating of a heart—the heart of a conquering darkness. It was a moment of triumph for the wilderness, an invading and vengeful
rush which, it seemed to me, I would have to keep back alone
for the salvation of another soul. . . . I rang the bell before a ma-
hogany door on the first floor, and while I waited he seemed to
stare at me out of the glassy panel—stare with that wide and
immense stare embracing, condemning, loathing all the universe. I seemed to hear the whispered cry, "The horror! The
horror!"

Joseph Conrad, *Heart of Darkness.*

physical danger; and he reacts with poise and determination
in defending his boat and humanely scattering his attackers.
Though frightened by the savages, he is sufficiently equipped,
morally and psychologically, to handle himself heroically in a
conventional sense. He even makes statements unthinkably
daring to a traditional hero like Robinson Crusoe. Commenting on the savages at one point, for example, he says:

> They howled and leaped, and spun, and made horrid faces;
> but what thrilled you was just the thought of their humanity
> —like yours—the thought of your remote kinship with this
> wild and passionate uproar. Ugly. Yes, it was ugly enough; but
> if you were man enough you would admit to yourself that

there was in you just the faintest trace of a response to the terrible frankness of that noise, a dim suspicion of there being a meaning in it which you—you so remote from the night of first ages—could comprehend.

This is just one example of Marlow's wonderful capacity for both sympathy and resilience. But ultimately this capacity relies upon a system of defense Marlow often exhibits when confronted with danger. At one point, he comments ironically about the cannibals, when their leader expresses a special interest in the savages along the river bank, "I would no doubt have been properly horrified, had it not occurred to me that he and his chaps must be very hungry." Marlow here may be mocking his own sense of "propriety" ("It takes a man all his inborn strength to fight hunger properly"), but in doing so, he also takes refuge in the cannibals' moral logic, as he sees it, because, while founded upon different (and at this point, humorously justifiable) premises from his own ideology, it is logical nonetheless. In fact, their moral logic may resemble ours, if we are honest enough to see the connections: if you are hungry, you must eat; if you are accustomed to eating men, you crave human flesh. There is more sense to this reasoning than there is to the mindless plotting of the company people. What really distinguishes between Marlow's reaction to the savages and the fear of the wilderness is the way he can extend the logic of his imagination but cannot contradict it. His mind is large enough to accommodate the rationale behind cannibalism, because he can make connections between it and his own way of thinking. But he cannot handle the strain of paradox, the horror that "the earth seemed unearthly," the inability to make any imaginative contact with his experience whatsoever.

Next to the fear of such an imaginative failure, Marlow welcomes the usual horrors, "the usual sense of commonplace, deadly danger, the possibility of a sudden onslaught and massacre . . . which pacified me, in fact, so much, that I did not raise alarm." These are dangers he can picture, can create images about in his imagination; and such image-making, as in the metaphors of light and darkness in the following passage, are essential to him. Commenting upon the human skulls surrounding the hut of Kurtz, Marlow says: "After all, that was only a savage sight, while I seemed at one bound to have been transported into some lightless region of subtle horrors, where pure, uncomplicated savagery was a positive relief, being something that had a right to exist—obviously—in the sunshine." This statement does not, of course, imply that Marlow is not upset by "pure, uncomplicated savagery," but that his heroism is large enough to reinforce him against his fears. It is Marlow's conscious mind, his marvelous ability to see connections, to make distinctions, to assimilate alien ideas . . . which is his most impressive quality. But this rationality, this ability to "[keep his] head pretty well," as he says of himself in contrast to Kurtz, is also like the rationality of Crusoe and his fictional descendents: it is used, in effect, as a verbal and psychological defense against fear. Marlow's irony, like the irony and sarcasm he directs against the company people, allows him to define, order, and evaluate his experiences—so long as he is not dealing with the wilderness itself.

MARLOW IS MORE THAN A MERE VOYAGER

Marlow's achievement as a heroic figure is perhaps best measured by the way that he . . . is not simply a voyager but a "wanderer," an observer, a cultural commentator whose sense of himself is born out of a highly sophisticated moral consciousness that may at times distance itself from and bear witness to the culture that formed it. But because Marlow's imagination seems to rely upon his ability to make analogies between what is familiar to him and what is unknown, in understanding what happens to him in "Heart of Darkness," we might appeal to the general logical precept that all analogies ultimately break down. Marlow is able to compare the natives' drums to Christian church bells, their demonstrations and dances to "an enthusiastic outbreak in a madhouse." But the wilderness is more than the savages—it is the darkness that Marlow constantly invokes, the darkness within which the devices of analogy fail. And because Marlow's entire cultural experience is inadequate as a vehicle for further analogies, we might say that both Marlow's language and his culture share the same fate. Together they represent the limitations of man's consciousness and rationality and the irrelevance of morality in the darkness that is beyond the inventions of man.

If Marlow is going to continue to live as a moral being, he must, once again, shelter himself from the wilderness within the limitations of order and coherence made possible by his conscious mind. It is a kind of willful self-delusion that permits him to escape Kurtz's fate. As in *The Nigger of the "Narcissus,"* language is associated with artifice and deception, with a contrived order. It is the counterfeit of some unrealized truth that would assert "life" against the apparent chaos of the wilderness. In "Heart of Darkness," as in *The Nigger,* the idea of a "lie" has a special meaning to it: "There is a taint of death, a flavour of mortality in lies," Marlow says, "—which is exactly what I hate and detest in the world —what I want to forget." After these two stories, there is only one way to read this statement so that its association between mortality and lies will make sense. All things human are lies—culture, morality, social order—because they are evasions of the darkness. The idea is explicitly stated in one of the letters I quoted in chapter 1, "Our refuge is in stupidity, in drunkenness of all kinds, in lies, in beliefs, in murder, thieving, reforming, in negation, in contempt—each man according to the promptings of his own particular devil." After "Heart of Darkness" it should be clearer why this catalogue of human activities is so varied and so inclusive: it is a condemnation of mortality itself. Yet, if man wants to escape lies, as Marlow wants to, he must follow Kurtz into self-obliteration. Without lies, human life is impossible; the order which is essential to it could not exist. Hence Marlow by the end of the tale must live with the knowledge that he too has to be a liar in order to survive.

MARLOW'S NEWFOUND WISDOM CHANGES HIM

The effect of Marlow's newfound wisdom upon his relationship to other people is something like that in Swift when Gulliver returns to England. Perhaps the best index to the changes in Marlow is the way his relationship develops to his peers, the members of his listening audience, in the increasing antagonism he feels towards them. His narrative asides begin as appeals for his audience's sympathy: "Do you see him? Do you see the story? Do you see anything? It seems to me I am trying to tell you a dream—making a vain attempt, because . . . No, it is impossible. We live as we dream—alone." Later these interruptions become more pointed, defensive, vindictive, as he compares his listeners to circus performers "on your respective tight-ropes—for what is it? half-a-crown a tumble," to which some insulted listener answers, "Try to be civil, Marlow." Marlow's immediate apology is colored with ironic indulgence, qualified mainly by including himself among the performers: "I beg your pardon. I forgot the heartache which makes up the rest of your price. . . . You do your tricks very well. And I didn't do so badly either." But the full measure of Marlow's disgust with himself, his listeners, and his entire society is unleashed in portrayals of society late in the novel that are shockingly warped if we are to compare them to his relatively harmless Dickensian caricatures[5] earlier:

> You can't understand. How could you?—with solid pavement under your feet, surrounded by kind neighbours ready to cheer you or to fall on you, stepping delicately between the butcher and the policeman, in the holy terror of scandal and gallows and lunatic asylums—how can you imagine what particular region of the first ages a man's untrammelled feet may take him into by the way of solitude—utter solitude without a policeman—by the way of silence—utter silence, where no warning voice of a kind neighbour can be heard whispering of public opinion?

The condemnation here is for both society's sordidness and for its vulgar comforts. It is an ugly picture to be sure, with its depiction of public gossip, institutionalized insanity, gruesome executions—a life that has its own risks and precariousness, its own horrors, a life in which even one's friends no more than "whisper" their warnings before they too may turn on one. This is a society that seems to prey upon itself. But—and this too is part of the condemnation—it is also a society that is perversely reassuring. At least one knows something about the risks, at least there are ways of deciding who one is and what one may expect. As long as one "steps delicately" enough, one may evade the gallows and the asylums where the Gullivers or the Marlows are more likely to end up. The price for social order is paid in honesty, courage, and some lingering notion of human decency.

"Heart of Darkness" perhaps should have ended on this note, for the vision the previous passage presents is consistent with the one developed throughout the story. Yet the story ends somewhat differently, with a twist on the idea of Marlow's humanity that also grows out of the movement in the story. The last scene in the book, the interview with Kurtz's Intended, may seem a kind of sentimental footnote. The woman is a saint, her suffering is more pathetic than

5. characters created by Charles Dickens in his novels

tragic, Marlow's kindness is in a sense another failure of his integrity, and Conrad himself seems to be reaching into his fantasies for ideal figures to shine amidst the ruins. But I find myself touched by this scene more than I am touched by Conrad's tribute at the end of *The Nigger of the "Narcissus,"* and I am not embarrassed about it here. The ironies of the scene are so blunt, yet so powerful. Marlow imaginatively brings the wilderness with him to the interview in a sequence that is cinematic in its flashbacks, juxtapositions, and superimpositions of sounds and images from the Congo: images of deepening darkness, sounds of the river, the drums, and the savages; and, as the pale, suffering woman extends her hands to greet Marlow, the image and voice of Kurtz himself crying, "The horror! the horror!" The wilderness pervades Marlow's being as he now knows it pervades the souls of all mankind, beneath the surface. As he offers his sympathy by endorsing the woman's platitudes ("His end . . . was in every way worthy of his life"), he writhes in their irony and hates himself for his lies. But then, in a wonderfully benign, generous, even tragic gesture on his part, Marlow admits that "My anger subsided before a feeling of infinite pity." And for the very fact that he does recoil from the lie he tells her ("The last word he pronounced was—your name."), he does not console himself by his consolation of the woman. He is able, instead, to temper his fear, his irony, his contempt for the weakness of mortals who need such lies with a marvelously moving assertion of life. Perhaps cowardly in one sense, this concession to humanity nevertheless is itself a kind of triumph.

There will henceforth be a difference in Conrad's fiction between what he lives with and what he lives by. Over truth he has chosen humanity—sadly, generously, knowingly. This is not heroism, it is sentimentality—but here, at least, it is so poignant, so fine.

Marlow's Failure of Will

Peter J. Glassman

According to Peter J. Glassman, Marlow's failure of will at the end of the novel to choose an authentic life over a convenient life of dimness and death is the novel's tragedy. Glassman maintains that Marlow learns openness and awareness from Kurtz and returns with a plan to live courageously and authentically, but the mundane activities of the city and the needs of Kurtz's Intended diminish his desire to follow his plan. Peter J. Glassman has taught English at Columbia University in New York, at Tulane University in New Orleans, Louisiana, and at the Chinese University of Hong Kong. He has published *J.S. Mill: The Evolution of a Genius* and *Fixity and Mobility: The Work of the Novel in Victorian England.*

Marlow leaves the Congo . . . with a programme. More than ever human life seems to him deadly and closed. But his own life has opened drastically, has yielded an example of authenticity and courage more authoritative by far than any other his career has extended—more authoritative, certainly, than the puerile fantasizing by which he began his great voyage. Kurtz has "enlarged" Marlow as his profession has not. If he cannot take Kurtz's "last stride," Marlow imagines that at least he can appreciate its edge. If he cannot be so "translucently pure" as Kurtz, he thinks at least to ape Kurtz's approaches to life, to imitate his allegiance to reality and his fidelity to experience. It is a worthy project, one which we expect him to undertake: surely he must respond in *some* way to the extraordinary "enlargement" the Congo has worked upon his habits and assumptions. (Marlow remarks, after all, that this "was the farthest point of navigation and the culminating point of my experience.")

Respond Marlow does, but with a curious quality of incertitude—as if his fervor were a matter more of fever than

From *Language and Being: Joseph Conrad and the Literature of Personality*, by Peter J. Glassman. New York: Columbia University Press, 1976. Reprinted by permission of the author.

of persuasion. It is not that he feels receptive to the ways of being Kurtz and the Congo have exposed, for he tells us that ordinary men repel him by their ignorance and banality:

> I found myself back in the sepulchral city resenting the sight of people hurrying through the streets to filch a little money from each other, to devour their infamous cookery, to gulp their unwholesome beer, to dream their insignificant and silly dreams. They trespassed upon my thoughts. They were intruders whose knowledge of life was to me an irritating pretence, because I felt so sure they could not possibly know the things I knew.

Trespassers, pretenders, intruders: they are worse than that, as Marlow by now ought to realize. For in their triviality they are terrified by legitimate authenticity—as they acknowledge by their compulsive need to domesticate, or even to arrogate to themselves, Marlow's whole memory of Kurtz's vigorous and particular life. Thus Marlow is positively flooded by weird agents of nonentity who crawl from every nook and cranny of the grave to snatch from him pieces of memory, fragments of assumption—portions of self. A ruddy-cheeked fool wants "certain 'documents,'" and insists that Kurtz was an explorer, no more than a geographer. A "senile" cousin of the deceased plunders letters and memos, and remarks of Kurtz that he was "essentially a great musician." A "furry" journalist walks off with Kurtz's Report (which in a deliberate and dreadful gesture of concession Marlow himself drastically expurgates), and describes Kurtz as an undiscriminating orator, a genius merely of demagogy.

MARLOW'S INSPIRATION WANES

What is called for in this contest for Kurtz's memory and Marlow's spirit is not repressed animadversion but passionate struggle. But what a wearied, private fight Marlow wages! I scorn thee, he whispers. I know more than all of you; I am more passionate, more alive, more actual, than any of you: "I had no particular desire to enlighten them, but I had some difficulty in restraining myself from laughing in their faces, so full of stupid importance." In this second and more momentous struggle for his moral life Marlow again can imagine only a gray and unexciting contest. "I had no particular desire. . . ." Can he not, like Kurtz, shriek out in one pure energy of integrity, Begone: "You with your little peddling notions—you are interfering with me"? For Marlow *is* being interfered with. Nonentity is reclaiming him, probing at his memories and passions till, little by little, they wear out and grow dim. And because his imagination "wanted soothing" he yields to the process. Because like a mindless Willems[1] he feels it less difficult to die than to live, he is pleased to surrender Kurtz's authenticity—and his own—to the obscene authority of quietude. Annihilate or be annihilated, Marlow. Exterminate all the brutes, or be exterminated oneself. Evidently it is one thing to know that most men's lives are insignificant and ridiculous, another to defend one's own. . . .

Marlow is so anxious to return to his normal economy of self that he tries to consign his whole Congo experience, together with its implied burden of demand, "to that oblivion which is the last word of our common fate." But his taste of extremity will not yield to his apostate wish[2] for simplicity and ease. It is precisely the principle of such experience as Marlow has had that it is autonomous, that its very memory is more compelling than the impalpable appeal of extinction. Thus, even as Marlow knocks on The Intended's door, even as he demands admission, as it were, to her uncomplicated sarcophagus of nonentity, his "expanded" consciousness makes a desperate gesture of revolt, a final, ungoverned appeal for the authority of life:

> I thought his memory was like the other memories of the dead that accumulate in every man's life; . . . but before the high and ponderous door, between the tall houses of a street as still and decorous as a well-kept alley in a cemetery, I had a vision of him on a stretcher, opening his mouth voraciously, as if to devour all the earth with all its mankind. He lived then before me; he lived as much as he had ever lived. . . .

And with him lives Marlow's memory of passionate and particular life. With him lives unforgotten and undiminished Marlow's whole feeling for the "frightful realities" of sex and self, his whole ecstasy with unmediated being. Those "horned shapes" of long ago, that stirring "glow of fires"; Kurtz's "broken phrases," all "the tempestuous anguish of his soul." Try as he does, Marlow cannot dispose of the importunate claims of life. What little there is in him which needs perforce to Be will not let him:

> I rang the bell before a mahogany door on the first floor, and while I waited he seemed to stare at me out of the glassy

1. a character in Conrad's "An Outcast of the Islands" 2. desire to give up his cause

panel—stare with that wide and immense stare embracing, condemning, loathing all the universe. I seemed to hear the whispered cry, "The horror! The horror!"

KURTZ'S MEMORY KEEPS MARLOW ALIVE

Kurtz still acts here as Marlow's agent of opinion; and Marlow does "sum up" and judge by an hysterical hallucination. But however conceived, the judgment of censure Marlow imagines stands as an occasion of crisis in his life, and of climax in *Heart of Darkness*. Always before *Heart of Darkness* has understood Marlow earlier than he has understood himself: although he invariably discovers those failures of his attitude or action by which the novel defines him, Marlow never before has been able to perceive the inadequacy of one of his "steps" in time to struggle against it. But here for the first time Marlow has comprehended, even imitated, Kurtz. For the first time he has achieved some knowledge of himself—achieved it, like Kurtz, in time to use it, in time to identify and control "that inappreciable moment of time in which we step over the threshold of the invisible." By understanding as he has that what he is *about* to do is "horrible," by understanding that "all the universe" is contemptible, Marlow has described for himself something of the openness and opportunity he has admired about Kurtz's life. For, like Kurtz, Marlow has compelled his life to submit to his own control, to yield to the severe "threshold" of free choice. He has achieved an authenticity of his own: like Kurtz, he has "kicked himself loose of the earth." Indeed, by so coherently conceiving the consequences of what he is about to do, Marlow at last establishes his life as a self, his right and power to make, like Kurtz, an organized choice between the opposed claims of opposite ways of being.

The novel's center of authority, then, has shifted—has passed in this great moment of unresisted self-contempt from the dead Kurtz to the living Marlow. For the first time in his life Marlow is not the victim of his novel's opinion, but its source, agent, and hero.

But if he has opened his life, Marlow cannot save it. It is the tragedy of *Heart of Darkness* that Marlow cannot engage his "inappreciable moment" of choice, that he can offer no more efficient struggle against his terrible taste for dimness and death than to inveigh against himself in hysterical whispers of self-hatred and despair. "The horror! The horror!"

Fully certain that what he is about to do is grievously wrong—believing, indeed, that he does not wish to do it!—Marlow rings The Intended's bell, tells his famous lies, perpetuates and thus enters into that absurd woman's frightful compact with ignorance, vapidity, and death. A "horror" indeed, Marlow manages this definitive occasion of choice as he has all the others in his life—by shying from extremity, by stepping back from that "threshold of the invisible" which by any other name is character.

In his habitual way Marlow protests that he had no choice. How, he pleads, could I *not* tell those lies? To disclose to that "guileless, profound, confident, and trustful" creature the brutal truth about her Kurtz, about human life, surely "would have been too dark—too dark altogether." Maybe so, if Marlow's humanity were all that were at issue here. But what in fact has been at issue, as Marlow himself well knows, is Marlow's whole moral life, his final response of character to the great "enlargement" Kurtz and the Congo have worked upon the range of his assumptions and experience. His hedging notwithstanding, Marlow fully understands that he has been at Kurtz's edge, that he has involved himself in a primal and permanent choice between two modes of being, two versions of experience, two standards of self:

> I saw her and [Kurtz] in the same instant of time—his death and her sorrow—I saw her sorrow in the very moment of his death. Do you understand? I saw them together—I heard them together. She had said, with a deep catch of the breath, "I have survived" while my strained ears seemed to hear distinctly, mingled with her tone of despairing regret, the summing up whisper of his eternal condemnation.

The Intended or Kurtz. Her sorrow or his life; her frightened separation from experience or his desperate wish to be; her empty, institutional "survival" or his triumphant death.

Poor Marlow! "More than a year" after leaving the Congo he is an unchanged man. Once again—once for all, conclusively—he has felt life to be impalpable, gray, less attractive than the undemanding release of endless nonentity and regret. No wonder he feels "a sensation of panic." He has stepped over his threshold at last—has stepped with the prophetess of his kind "beyond the threshold of an eternal darkness," beyond the bound of the stallion's appeal. Here, where life is soothing but dim, Marlow finally has his figurative character, his awful "crop of unextinguishable regrets." Here, terribly preserved from the demands and dues of a fiercer self, Marlow is free to struggle forever after the ecstasy and energy of that purer life he has refused. Free, too, to sum up and to judge the mode of unbeing he has affirmed; to regard with horror the closed shapes of his decision against life; to detest himself forever as "a trifle" who feared to become either a monster or a saint.

It is Marlow's last gesture of integrity that he permits his narrative to end, like his moral life, in ellipses. He could do nothing else, for he leaves *Heart of Darkness* an emptied and helpless man. Mean, secretive, full of furious wrath against a self which he cannot change, Marlow leaves his novel not opened to experience but recoiling from it; not opened to human life but afraid of it, incapable of it, demonstrably opposed to it. . . .

MARLOW ENDS IN SUFFERING, ISOLATION, AND SELF-CONTEMPT

What identity of self Marlow discovers in *Heart of Darkness* proceeds, then, from no normally human assembly of energies, functions, or joys, but from his extreme self-hatred: by detesting who he is, Marlow at last locates who he is: No doubt it is important to describe oneself, but obviously *this* sort of moral distinctness suggests only a theoretical value. For although it is true that other novels force their best people to feel painfully about themselves, they do so because they believe that self contempt may provoke corrections of character, or changes of personality, or adjustments of difficulty. Marlow, though, gains nothing from his self-contempt. His awful abuse of himself does not lead to a freer culture of understanding, nor to a larger sentiment of existence, nor even to a deeper emotive power. He merely suffers. He is more particularized at the end of his novel than before his voyage to the Congo; but he is no more authoritative morally, and certainly he is less happy. His "enlargement" yields him more contempt for himself but not more character or life.

It is for this reason that *Heart of Darkness* ends so very suddenly. "Marlow ceased, and sat apart, indistinct and silent, in the pose of a meditating Buddha." Marlow stops talking so abruptly and finally because in every sense which matters he *has* ceased. Reduced to one sensation of desperate contempt, no longer an affective creature, Marlow has become a sum of pain, a dim little duchy of suffering. Indistinct, stilled, estranged from other men, himself, and all pleasurable life, he completes his career as he began it, in a desolate agony of isolation. . . .

Marlow's story has eroded all the narrator's first, uninformed serenity about men, life, the river, the world, himself. Now that he has heard *Heart of Darkness* the narrator feels what the novel expects we shall feel: that human life is in all things grim; that one is oneself unformed and unlovely, not deeply alive; that all the waterways and promontories of the world promise neither variety nor pleasure, but only "an immense darkness" of nonentity and despair. In their tonality of distress, their dreadful suggestion of fear and disgust, the narrator's last words define a completed sympathy with Marlow, an understanding of his misery so extreme as to imply communion with it.

Like Marlow, then, the narrator defines himself by his aversion to experience and his isolation from it. So, too, does *Heart of Darkness* define itself—and its tortured maker. "I know well that I will never be anything." Remedy or tragedy, *Heart of Darkness* is certainly autobiography, the most forbidding autobiography, I daresay, in English. (No other autobiography can have had less faith in the authority of the self!)

CHAPTER 3

Conrad's Style and Methods

READINGS ON
HEART OF DARKNESS

Multiple Narrators in *Heart of Darkness*

Jakob Lothe

Jakob Lothe explains the effect of Conrad's two first-person narrators: the anonymous narrator and Marlow. Lothe points out that the narrator is less knowledgeable than Marlow and argues that Marlow serves as a distancing device. Lothe also argues that the two narrators play off of one another to increase the impact and suggestiveness of Marlow's words. Jakob Lothe teaches comparative literature at the University of Oslo. He is the author of *Conrad's Narrative Method* and editor of *Conrad in Scandinavia*.

Conradian narrative is not only exceptionally sophisticated and varied but also remarkably productive thematically. In common with all major writers, Conrad's fictional content is inextricable from narrative presentation. To make this point is not to regard the concept of content as unimportant. It is to stress that the rhetorical persuasiveness, ideological tension, dramatic intensity, and continuing interest and relevance of Conrad's fictional vision depend upon and are indeed generated and shaped by diverse and original narrative techniques. It follows that a discussion of Conradian narrative is a substantial critical venture. This treatment will focus on a selection of particularly important constituent aspects of Conrad's narrative strategies. . . .

The concept of narrative is understood inclusively: it both designates and incorporates the various constituent aspects of Conrad's literary world. This world, which the narrative serves to present and shape, is a fictional one: rather than recording what has happened, it dramatizes—on a more generalized and less explicit level—what *could* happen. As the historical author, Conrad is a *writer*—a designer of a fictional universe. While Conrad remains outside this universe,

Excerpted from Jakob Lothe, "Conradian Narrative," in *The Cambridge Companion to Joseph Conrad*, edited by J.H. Stape. Copyright © 1996 by Cambridge University Press. Reprinted by permission of Cambridge University Press. *Endnotes and sources referenced in the original have been omitted in this reprint.*

'traces' of his views, doubts, fears, hopes, and so forth are observable in the fiction he produced. Such traces can be subsumed under the abstract concept of the implied author, the author's second self constructed from the text's narrative discourse. Interestingly, when we refer to 'Conrad' we often think of Conrad as the implied author, that is, as represented by, or emerging through, his fiction. . . . Furthermore, the concept of author, whether historical or implied, needs to be related to that of the narrator. As an integral part of the fictional creation, the narrator, or the combination of narrators, is the author's primary means of shaping a text, which consists of the activities and functions the narrator is made to perform. In Conrad's fiction these functions are, in most cases, crucially important for presenting the fictional content. . . .

THE KINDS OF NARRATORS CONRAD USES

While narrators can be variously grouped and re-grouped, depending on one's criteria, the most essential distinction to draw—generally as well as in Conrad—is that between third- and first-person narrators. . . . Conrad's fiction confirms the validity of this critical distinction. Conradian narrative can be consistently and intensely first-person—as in *The Shadow-Line*—wide-rangingly third-person—as in *Nostromo*—or can attempt to combine the two main variants— as in *Lord Jim*. Although the gains of such a combination are potentially considerable, it also presents the author with narrative problems. . . .

The fiction Conrad wrote from 1897 to 1900 was crucially important for the development of his narrative method: following *The Nigger of the 'Narcissus'* he published, in rapid succession, such major works as 'An Outpost of Progress', 'Heart of Darkness', and *Lord Jim*. 'An Outpost of Progress', whose third-person narrative anticipates *Nostromo* rather than 'Heart of Darkness', is an impressive feat of narrative concentration. . . .

If a distinctive feature of 'An Outpost of Progress' is the focus on a particular situation, closely related to a rendering of monotony, futility, and absurdity, the short story is also characterized by an accumulative thematic suggestiveness— of questions Conrad was to explore further in 'Heart of Darkness', in which an oblique narrative technique proves strikingly congenial with the novella's thematics. . . .

MARLOW AS NARRATOR HELPS CONRAD DISTANCE HIMSELF

The introduction of Marlow marks a turning-point in Conradian narrative. This shift is not merely technical, but intimately connected with Conrad's uncertainty and experimentation as a writer of fiction. [In *Joseph Conrad: A Chronicle* critic] Zdzislaw Najder helpfully comments on Marlow's importance for Conrad's writing:

> Marlow, a model English gentleman, ex-officer of the merchant marine, was the embodiment of all that Conrad would wish to be if he were to become completely anglicized. And since that was not the case, and since he did not quite share his hero's point of view, there was no need to identify himself with Marlow, either emotionally or intellectually. Thanks to Marlow's duality, Conrad could feel solidarity with, and a sense of belonging to, England by proxy, at the same time maintaining a distance such as one has toward a creation of one's imagination. Thus, Conrad, although he did not permanently resolve his search for a consistent consciousness of self-identity, found an integrating point of view that enabled him, at last, to break out of the worst crisis of his writing career.

This comment is persuasive partly because of its implied suggestion that, for Conrad, Marlow is not only a main narrator and an important character, but a distancing device that helps the author control and shape his fictional material. In a classic essay ["Psychological Distance"] published as early as 1912, Edward Bullough regarded 'distance' as the quality that gives an expression aesthetic validity: 'Distancing means the separation of personal affections, whether idea or complex experience, from the concrete personality of the experience'. Thus understood, the concept serves to identify one of the most distinctive aspects of Conradian narrative. As far as Conrad is concerned, Bullough's general observation blends into the author's *need for distance* both from his fiction and, in a complex way, from his audience, in order to write at all.

The concept of distance needs, however, to be diversified to be helpful critically. The most important variants are temporal, spatial, and attitudinal distance. In 'Heart of Darkness', there is a significant temporal distance between Conrad's personal experience in the Congo in 1890, on which the fiction is based, and the time of the novella's writing approximately eight years later. There is also a very considerable spatial distance between London, the setting of the narrative act, and the Congo, the place of the main action. Finally, the temporal and spatial distances are related to the 'attitudinal' distance, the ideological perspectives of the narrator(s) and the implied author. This last variant is the most complex because it is more closely connected with the varying levels of insight of the implied author, the narrator, and character, and because it is, as a critical metaphor, related to the reader's interpretive activity.

A good illustration of modulations of distance is provided by the opening of 'Heart of Darkness'. The novella begins by introducing us to a narrative setting that establishes a peculiarly static frame around the main action. A group of five men are aboard a cruising yawl, waiting for the turn of the tide:

> The sea-reach of the Thames stretched before us like the beginning of an interminable waterway. In the offing the sea and the sky were welded together without a joint, and in the luminous space the tanned sails of the barges drifting up with the tide seemed to stand still in red clusters of canvas sharply peaked, with gleams of varnished sprits.

The visual qualities of this introductory description resemble those often referred to in discussions of Conrad's literary impressionism. Suggesting a first-person narrative, the pronoun 'us' refers to the five characters aboard the *Nellie*. One of them is Marlow; however, not Marlow but an anonymous first-person narrator is speaking here. This frame narrator introduces us to the setting of the novella as well as to Marlow as the main narrator. When Marlow is duly introduced and embarks on his tale, the function of the frame narrator becomes more complex, since he also becomes a *narratee*[1] in the group Marlow addresses. To put this another way: in accordance with the narrative convention employed, the frame narrator functions first as a narratee, and then as a first-person narrator relaying Marlow's story to the reader. . . .

THE FUNCTIONS OF THE ANONYMOUS FRAME NARRATOR AND MARLOW

In the classic frame narrative the frame narrator is often the most authoritative and knowledgeable of the narrators. This is not so in 'Heart of Darkness'. For although the frame narrator passes on Marlow's story and appears to be reliable, his insights are distinctly inferior to Marlow's. A second example will illustrate this point. Having finished his intro-

---

1. The narratee is the agent who is at least implicitly, and often also explicitly, addressed by the narrator.

THE FRAME NARRATOR'S ROLE

As the story opens, the narrator sets the stage and the tone and introduces fellow sailors who tell yarns on board.

Between us there was, as I have already said somewhere, the bond of the sea. Besides holding our hearts together through long periods of separation, it had the effect of making us tolerant of each other's yarns—and even convictions. The Lawyer—the best of old fellows—had, because of his many years and many virtues, the only cushion on deck, and was lying on the only rug. The Accountant had brought out already a box of dominoes, and was toying architecturally with the bones. Marlow sat cross-legged right aft, leaning against the mizzen-mast. He had sunken cheeks, a yellow complexion, a straight back, an ascetic aspect, and, with his arms dropped, the palms of hands outwards, resembled an idol. The director, satisfied the anchor had good hold, made his way aft and sat down amongst us. We exchanged a few words lazily. Afterwards there was silence on board the yacht. For some reason or other we did not begin that game of dominoes. We felt meditative, and fit for nothing but placid staring. The day was ending in a serenity of still and exquisite brilliance. The water shone pacifically; the sky, without a speck, was a benign immensity of unstained light; the very mist on the Essex marshes was like a gauzy and radiant fabric, hung from the wooded rises inland, and draping the low shores in diaphanous folds. Only the gloom to the west, brooding over the upper reaches, became more sombre every minute, as if angered by the approach of the sun.

And at last, in its curved and imperceptible fall, the sun sank low, and from glowing white changed to a dull red without rays and without heat, as if about to go out suddenly, stricken to death by the touch of that gloom brooding over a crowd of men.

Joseph Conrad, *Heart of Darkness.*

ductory description, the narrator exclaims: 'What greatness had not floated on the ebb of that river into the mystery of an unknown earth! . . . The dreams of men, the seed of commonwealths, the germs of empires'. Isolated from its context, the exclamation sounds like a piece of imperialistic rhetoric. This impression increases the impact and suggestiveness of Marlow's first words: 'And this also . . . has been one of the dark places of the earth'.

This narrative variation is one of the most effective in all of Conrad's fiction. Marlow's remark exposes the relative naïveté and limited insight of the frame narrator and pre-figures the complex, sombre implications of the tale he is about to tell. The comment anticipates his later reflections on the arrival of the Romans in Britain, 'nineteen hundred years ago—the other day'. For the Romans, Marlow plausibly goes on to suggest, Britain must have seemed an inhospitable wilderness at 'the very end of the world'. Additionally, it is indicative of the extraordinary narrative economy of 'Heart of Darkness' that Marlow's opening words also function as a prolepsis[2] of 'darkness', the text's central metaphor. Although the Romans 'were men enough to face the darkness . . . They were conquerors, and for that you want only brute force—nothing to boast of, when you have it, since your strength is just an accident arising from the weakness of others'. This generalizing statement obviously refers to the Romans, but also includes a proleptic reference to the narrative Marlow is just starting.

Suggesting that Marlow's level of insight is superior to that of the frame narrator, these brief observations also indicate some key characteristics of Marlow's first-person narrative: a reflective rhetoric designed to impress and persuade, a peculiar blend of personal and intellectual curiosity, and a tendency to generalize on the basis of individual experience. Conrad thus uses two first-person narrators in 'Heart of Darkness', and the effect of Marlow's narrative is inseparable from the function of the frame narrator.

THE EFFECTS OF USING TWO NARRATORS

The use of a narrator is a distancing device, and 'Heart of Darkness' accentuates the distancing process by the use of two narrators rather than one. At the same time, the novella is also a good example of a text where distancing narrative devices paradoxically increase the reader's attention and interest. Conrad effectively exploits the conventional or common character of the frame narrator to make Marlow's story more plausible. The frame narrative manipulates the reader into a position resembling that of the frame narrator *as narratee*, a position distinguished by a meditative but broadly accepting response to the disillusioned insights of Marlow's story. This effect is particularly evident in the novella's last paragraph, which is spoken by the frame narrator. Echoing

2. Prolepsis is any narrative maneuver that narrates or evokes *in advance* an event that will take place later.

the numerous references to 'darkness', its concluding words —'immense darkness'—repeat Marlow's last words in the paragraph above.

In 'Heart of Darkness', there is a productive correlation [between] Marlow's first-person narration, which takes the form of an ordering and existentially motivated re-experience, and that of the frame narrator, which proceeds from an unexpected involvement and a surprising understanding. The frame narrator's involvement increases as a result of the impressionist narrative he himself transmits. [In *Conrad in the Nineteenth Century,* critic] Ian Watt has coined the term delayed decoding to describe this aspect of Conrad's impressionist narrative: through delayed decoding the author attempts 'to present a sense impression and to withhold naming it or explaining its meaning until later. . . . This takes us directly into the observer's consciousness at the very moment of the perception, before it has been translated into its cause'. Conrad used this device prior to 'Heart of Darkness', but one of its notable manifestations is Marlow's confusion when his boat is attacked just below Kurtz's station. Only later does he discover the cause of the various odd changes he observes: 'Arrows, by Jove! We were being shot at!' The concept of delayed decoding is probably most helpful in describing relatively simple instances of temporarily inexplicable impressions and occurrences. A larger problem—Marlow's impression of Kurtz, for example—is not decoded. . . .

The relationship between Conrad and his narrators is complicated, but it surely does not follow that it is unimportant. In Conrad's fiction, the narrator's relationship with the story told cannot be separated from the author's relationship with his work—and, by implication, with the world that the work portrays.

Conrad's Impressionism

Ian Watt

Ian Watt writes about the way Conrad details what a character sees and experiences as events are happening and follows with an explanation of the causes of events and the meaning of scenes. Watt calls this technique delayed decoding. Ian Watt has taught English at Stanford University in California. He is the author of *The Rise of the Novel: Studies in Defoe, Richardson and Fielding; Four Western Myths: Faust, Don Quixote, Don Juan, and Robinson Crusoe;* and a two-volume critical study of Conrad.

Conrad's most helpful comment on the method of *Heart of Darkness* occurs very early in the story, where the primary narrator explains that the meanings of Marlow's tales are characteristically difficult to encompass:

> The yarns of seamen have a direct simplicity, the whole meaning of which lies within the shell of a cracked nut. But Marlow was not typical (if his propensity to spin yarns be excepted), and to him the meaning of an episode was not inside like a kernel but outside, enveloping the tale which brought it out only as a glow brings out a haze, in the likeness of one of these misty halos that sometimes are made visible by the spectral illumination of moonshine. . . .

The sensory quality of the metaphor, the mist and haze, is essentially impressionist.

Mist or haze is a very persistent image in Conrad. It appeared as soon as he began to write: there was an "opaline haze" over the Thames on the morning when he had recalled Almayer[1]; and the original Olmeijer had first come into Conrad's view through the morning mists of Borneo. In *Heart of Darkness* the fugitive nature and indefinite contours of haze are given a special significance by the primary narrator; he warns us that Marlow's tale will be not centered on,

---

1. reference to *Almayer's Folly,* Conrad's novel published in 1895

Excerpted from *Conrad in the Nineteenth Century,* by Ian Watt (Berkeley and Los Angeles: University of California Press). Copyright © 1979 by Ian Watt. Reprinted by permission of the publisher. *Footnotes in the original have been omitted in this reprint.*

but surrounded by, its meaning; and this meaning will be only as fitfully and tenuously visible as a hitherto unnoticed presence of dust particles and water vapour in a space that normally looks dark and void. This in turn reminds us that one of the most characteristic objections to Impressionist painting was that the artist's ostensive "subject" was obscured by his representation of the atmospheric conditions through which it was observed. [French impressionist] Claude Monet, for instance, said of the critics who mocked him: "Poor blind idiots. They want to see everything clearly, even through the fog!" For Monet, the fog in a painting, like the narrator's haze, is not an accidental interference which stands between the public and a clear view of the artist's "real" subject: the conditions under which the viewing is done are an essential part of what the pictorial—or the literary—artist sees and therefore tries to convey.

A similar idea, expressed in a similar metaphor, occurs twenty years later in [British novelist] Virginia Woolf's classic characterization of "Modern Fiction" (1919). . . . Virginia Woolf finally affirms, "Life is not a series of gig lamps symmetrically arranged; life is a luminous halo, a semitransparent envelope surrounding us from the beginning of consciousness to the end."

The implications of these images of haze and halo for the essential nature of modern fiction are made somewhat clearer by the analogy of French Impressionist painting, and by the history of the word impressionism.

As a specifically aesthetic term, "Impressionism" was apparently put into circulation in 1874 by a journalist, Louis Leroy, to ridicule the affronting formlessness of the pictures exhibited at the Salon des Indépendants, and particularly of Claude Monet's painting entitled "Impression: Sunrise." In one way or another all the main Impressionists made it their aim to give a pictorial equivalent of the visual sensations of a particular individual at a particular time and place. . . .

The history of the words "impression" and "impressionism" in English embodies a more general aspect of the long process whereby in every domain of human concerns the priority passed from public systems of belief—what all men know—to private views of reality—what the individual sees. . . .

By [the 1890s] the main English usage of the term "impressionism" was in reference to the French school of painters, and to their English counterparts who came to the fore with the foundation of the New English Art Club in 1886. As in France, the term was very quickly extended to ways of writing which were thought to possess the qualities popularly attributed to the painters—to works that were spontaneous and rapidly executed, that were vivid sketches rather than detailed, finished, and premeditated compositions. The literary use of the term remained even more casual and descriptive; although [American novelist] Stephen Crane was widely categorised as an "impressionist," and in 1898 a reviewer of Conrad's first collection of short stories, *Tales of Unrest*, described him as an "impressionistic realist," there was little talk of impressionism as a literary movement until considerably later. . . .

Conrad certainly knew something about pictorial and literary impressionism, but the indications are that his reactions were predominantly unfavourable. Conrad's tastes in painting, as in music, were distinctly old-fashioned; he apparently disliked Van Gogh and Cézanne, and the only painter he ever mentioned as a model for his own writing was the peasant realist Jean-François Millet: in a letter to [writer and friend Arthur Thomas] Quiller-Couch, Conrad wrote "it has been my desire to do for seamen what Millet (if I dare pronounce the name of that great man and good artist in this connection) has done for peasants." As to literary impressionism, at the very least Conrad probably read a mildly derogatory article on "The Philosophy of Impressionism," which appeared in *Blackwood's Magazine* in May 1898. . . .

CONRAD'S EMPHASIS ON THE INDIVIDUAL'S SENSE IMPRESSIONS

Perhaps the most distinctive quality of Conrad's own writing, like Crane's and unlike [Conrad's friend, novelist Ford Madox] Ford's, is its strong visual sense; and Conrad's insistence in the preface to *The Nigger of the "Narcissus"* that art depends for its success on an "impression conveyed through the senses," is to that extent wholly consistent with impressionist doctrine. So, indeed, is much of the narrative itself, whose technique constitutes an original kind of multiple visual impressionism. This was immediately recognized by [novelist] Arnold Bennett when he read *The Nigger of the "Narcissus"*; he wrote admiringly to [novelist] H.G. Wells in 1897 asking: "Where did the man pick up . . . that *synthetic* way of gathering up a general impression and flinging it at you?"

Heart of Darkness is essentially impressionist in one very special and yet general way: it accepts, and indeed in its very form asserts, the bounded and ambiguous nature of individual understanding; and because the understanding sought is of an inward and experiential kind, we can describe the basis of its narrative method as subjective moral impressionism. Marlow's story explores how one individual's knowledge of another can mysteriously change the way in which he sees the world as a whole, and the form of *Heart of Darkness* proposes that so ambitious an enterprise can only be begun through one man trying to express his most inward impressions of how deeply problematic is the quest for—to use [novelist and critic Walter] Pater's terms—"an outer world, and of other minds.". . .

Heart of Darkness embodies more thoroughly than any previous fiction the posture of uncertainty and doubt; one of Marlow's functions is to represent how much a man cannot know; and he assumes that reality is essentially private and individual—work, he comments, gives you "the chance to find yourself. Your own reality—for yourself, not for others— what no other man can ever know. They can only see the mere show, and never can tell what it really means."

The other most distinctively impressionist aspect of Conrad's narrative method concerns his approach to visual description; and this preoccupation with the problematic relation of individual sense impressions to meaning is shown most clearly in one of the minor innovations of his narrative technique.

Long before *Heart of Darkness* Conrad seems to have been trying to find ways of giving direct narrative expression to the way in which the consciousness elicits meaning from its perceptions. One of the devices that he hit on was to present a sense impression and to withhold naming it or explaining its meaning until later; as readers we witness every step by which the gap between the individual perception and its cause is belatedly closed within the consciousness of the protagonist.

In both "The Idiots" and "An Outpost of Progress" the climax of the story is presented in this way. Thus in "The Idiots," when Susan Bacadou jumps over the edge of the cliffs to her death, a seaweed-gatherer merely sees that she "at once vanished before his eyes, as if the islet itself had swerved aside from under her feet." This takes us directly into the observer's consciousness at the very moment of the perception, before it has been translated into its cause, into the term death or suicide, which make the sense-events of the outside world intelligible and communicable to the observer. . . .

CONRAD'S METHOD: DELAYED DECODING

This narrative device may be termed delayed decoding, since it combines the forward temporal progression of the mind, as it receives messages from the outside world, with the much slower reflexive process of making out their meaning. . . .

By the time Conrad came to write *Heart of Darkness*, then, he had developed one narrative technique which was the verbal equivalent of the impressionist painter's attempt to render visual sensation directly. Conrad presented the protagonist's immediate sensations, and thus made the reader aware of the gap between impression and understanding; the delay in bridging the gap enacts the disjunction between the event and the observer's trailing understanding of it. In *Heart of Darkness* Conrad uses the method for the most dramatic action of the story, when Marlow's boat is attacked, just below Kurtz's station. Marlow, terrified of going aground, is anxiously watching the cannibal sounding in the bows just below him: "I was looking down at the sounding-pole, and feeling much annoyed to see at each try a little more of it stick out of that river, when I saw my poleman give up the business suddenly, and stretch himself flat on the deck, without even taking the trouble to haul his pole in.". . .

The effect is duplicated: "At the same time the fireman, whom I could also see below me, sat down abruptly before his furnace and ducked his head. I was amazed." Only now does the cause of these odd changes in posture begin to emerge: "Then I had to look at the river mighty quick, because there was a snag in the fairway. Sticks, little sticks, were flying about—thick: they were whizzing before my nose, dropping below me, striking behind me against my pilot-house." But it is only when Marlow has finished attending to his duty as captain, and negotiated the next snag, that his understanding can finally decode the little sticks:

"We cleared the snag clumsily. Arrows, by Jove! We were being shot at!"

Meanwhile the pilgrims, and, to Marlow's fury, even his helmsman, have started "squirting lead" into the bush. Marlow is navigating and catching occasional glimpses of "vague forms of men" through the shutterhole of the pilot-house, when his attention is suddenly deflected:

> Something big appeared in the air before the shutter, the rifle went overboard, and the man stepped back swiftly, looked at me over his shoulder in an extraordinary, profound, familiar manner, and fell upon my feet. The side of his head hit the wheel twice, and the end of what appeared a long cane clattered round and knocked over a little camp-stool. It looked as though after wrenching that thing from somebody ashore he had lost his balance in the effort. The thin smoke had blown away, we were clear of the snag, and looking ahead I could see that in another hundred yards or so I would be free to sheer off, away from the bank; but my feet felt so warm and wet that I had to look down. The man had rolled on his back and stared straight up at me; both his hands clutched that cane. It was the shaft of a spear . . . He looked at me anxiously, gripping the spear like something precious, with an air of being afraid I would try to take it away from him.

A third sudden and unfamiliar action is enacted through the protagonist's consciousness, and the delay in his decoding of it makes the reader simultaneously experience horror and sardonic amusement. Amusement, because we feel a certain patronising contempt for those who do not understand things as quickly as we do, and because there is a gruesome comedy in the mere visual impression of the helmsman's "air of being afraid I would try to take [the spear] away from him." This macabre note has already been prepared for: if the poleman lies down, and then the fireman sits down, it is only natural that Marlow should assume that the dead helmsman's recumbent posture must be just a third example of the crew's deserting their duty just for their personal safety.

Still, the passage is obviously not primarily comic. Conrad's main objective is to put us into intense sensory contact with the events; and this objective means that the physical impression must precede the understanding of cause. Literary impressionism implies a field of vision which is not merely limited to the individual observer, but is also controlled by whatever conditions—internal and external—prevail at the moment of observation. In narration the main equivalents to atmospheric interference in painting are the various factors which normally distort human perception, or which delay its recognition of what is most relevant and important. First of all, our minds are usually busy with other things—Marlow has a lot to do just then, and it is only natural that he should be annoyed by being faced with these three new interferences with his task of keeping the boat from disaster. Secondly, our interpretations of impressions are normally distorted by habitual expectations—Marlow perceives the unfamiliar arrows as familiar sticks. Lastly, we always have many more things in our range of vision than we can pay attention to, so that in a crisis we may miss the most important ones—in this case that the helmsman has been killed. Conrad's method reflects all these difficulties in translating perceptions into causal or conceptual terms. . . .

DELAYED DECODING ENGAGES THE READER IN THE EXPERIENCE

The device of delayed decoding simultaneously enacts the objective and the subjective aspects of moments of crisis. The method also has the more obvious advantage of convincing us of the reality of the experience which is being described; there is nothing suspiciously selective about the way it is narrated; while we read we are, as in life, fully engaged in trying to decipher a meaning out of a random and pell-mell bombardment of sense impressions. . . .

Conrad's device of delayed decoding represents an original narrative solution to the general problem of expressing the process whereby the individual's sensations of the external world are registered and translated into the causal and conceptual terms which can make them understandable to the observer and communicable to other people. More generally, Marlow's emphasis on the difficulty of understanding and communicating his own individual experience aligns *Heart of Darkness* with the subjective relativism of the impressionist attitude. Nevertheless, it is very unlikely that Conrad either thought of himself as an impressionist or was significantly influenced by the impressionist movement. Conrad wanted to pay as much attention to the inside as to the outside, to the meaning as to the appearance; and this is one of the reasons why, in the last analysis, he is so different both from the French Impressionists and from Pater, Crane, or Ford.

Behind this difference is another which gives a unique quality to the impressionist elements in Conrad. For Conrad, the world of the senses is not a picture but a presence. . . . Ramon Fernandez, in one of the very few indispensable essays on Conrad, remarks that his way of describing the external world is the exact opposite of traditional narrative description such as [French novelist Honoré de] Balzac's: Conrad's art, he writes, "does not trace the reality before the man, but the man before the reality; it evokes experiences in their subjective entirety because the impression is the equivalent of the entire perception, and because the whole man experiences it with all the powers of his being." Conrad's "great originality," Fernandez concludes, "is to have applied this impressionism to the knowledge of human beings."

The Rich Effects of Conrad's Style

Leo Gurko

Leo Gurko argues that Conrad's skillful selection of realistic details and his ability to evoke emotions create a spell in *Heart of Darkness*. Gurko illustrates his point by discussing various critical interpretations; a variety of themes, such as imperialism; a variety of methods, such as the contrast between Marlow and Kurtz; and the inclusion of both opposition and unity. Leo Gurko has taught English at Hunter College in New York and served as a publisher's reader for Macmillan. He is the author of *Joseph Conrad: Giant in Exile*, *The Two Lives of Joseph Conrad*, and *Ernest Hemingway and the Pursuit of Heroism*.

Marlow's journey into the unknown—the Congo had been acquired only recently by the Belgians and was still largely unexplored—has an air of tension and mystery throughout. Images of death appear almost from the start. Marlow signs up for a post as captain of a Congo river-steamer in Brussels, "a whited sepulchre" of a city. In the anteroom of the Company office sit two women in black, knitting, "guarding the door of Darkness." Marlow is made uneasy by the doctor who examines him: there is the odd procedure of taking his skull measurements, and the hints of mental changes caused by a sojourn in Africa. Even his aunt, who helped get him the job, adds to his disquiet when she naively insists that the Company's aim is to civilize the Congolese. By the time he leaves Europe, Marlow is in an unsettled state, with the queer feeling that he is an imposter, on his way not "to the centre of a continent" but to "the centre of the earth."

The trip down the African coast is equally unsettling. There is the fierce sun, the land glistening and dripping with steam, the "settlements no bigger than pinheads" on the

Reprinted from the Introduction, by Leo Gurko, to *Heart of Darkness*, by Joseph Conrad (Norwalk, CT: Heritage Press, 1969).

edge of "a colossal jungle" with names like Gran' Bassam and Little Popo, "names that seemed to belong to some sordid farce acted in front of a sinister back-cloth." A French warship stands offshore firing her guns at some invisible target inland. "In the empty immensity of earth, sky, and water, there she was, incomprehensible, firing into a continent." The insanity of this, the forbidding nature of the coastline, the "oily, languid" sea, intensify Marlow's sense of "vague and oppressive wonder."

By this time we are thoroughly under the spell of the narrative, with its brilliant selection of realistic detail while evoking meanings and emotions lying beneath the surface. All the celebrated journeys of literature exert this double hold, the recognizable outer layer of things so introduced as to arouse the deeper response. The two modern examples most familiar to Conrad, [Samuel Taylor Coleridge's] *The Rime of the Ancient Mariner* and [Herman Melville's] *Moby Dick*, reveal an identical grip on the duality of experience. *Heart of Darkness* follows the same pattern.

An Examination of Imperialism

In Africa, Marlow is shocked by the ravages of imperialism. He comes to a grove filled with dying Negroes, too broken in health to work on the chain gangs any longer. Farther on, at the Central Station, he meets the manager and his henchmen, crassly devoted to extracting as much ivory as possible out of the country: "To tear treasure out of the bowels of the earth was their desire, with no more moral purpose at the back of it than there is in burglars breaking into a safe." Their naked rapacity fills Marlow with loathing, and this quickens his interest in Kurtz, who had come to Africa with the "higher" aim of civilizing the natives and whom even his enemies acknowledge to be remarkable. He, too, is an imperialist trader—he sends out record-breaking quantities of ivory—but of a different sort, and Marlow is to be confronted with a "choice of nightmares," between the systems of value represented by the manager and by Kurtz. The need to choose forces a change of role on Marlow: he can no longer remain just an interested traveler; he becomes a moral participant.

In *Heart of Darkness*, as later in *Nostromo*, Conrad examines without prejudice the generally discredited process of imperialism. What redeems imperialism for Marlow, as for Conrad, is "an idea at the back of it; not a sentimental pretense but an idea." Kurtz has such an idea—to elevate the native—and the manager has not. Both are in the African darkness but on different levels of morality, and Marlow allies himself with Kurtz. If darkness it must be, it had better be Kurtz's. His at least has intelligence, a noble purpose, and a touch of grandeur, while the manager's is rooted in a grubby, mean spirited avarice. No matter that Kurtz, severely tempted, plunged into an abyss of degradation, that he engaged in abominable rites which Conrad, wisely, does not detail but alludes to with deliberate vagueness as "monstrous," "unspeakable," and "inconceivable." It is true that he allowed the tribesmen to deify him, killed natives and gruesomely impaled their heads on posts outside the Inner Station. Kurtz himself sums up his African career with his dying words, "The horror! the horror!" But if he has fallen, he has fallen from a great height, and Marlow finds in his fall a sign of his superiority. The manager, in contrast, has never left the ground, has never been motivated by an idea but only by a greedy appetite. He has, in fact, nowhere to fall to. Though Marlow embraces the inescapable darkness of life, it is a mark of his humanity that he retains his powers of discrimination within it.

MARLOW'S SELF-PRESERVATION CONTRASTED WITH KURTZ'S FAILURE

He discovers that it is possible to function in darkness without losing one's footing like Kurtz and falling into a bottomless pit, or existing, like the manager, without the slightest awareness of light. He sustains himself by continually making moral judgments about his experiences. He recognizes the absurd young Russian who is attached to Kurtz as an admirable incarnation of youthful adventurousness, just as he sees the manager's assistant, with his nose for influential connections back home, as a "papier-mâché Mephistopheles,[1]" a villain of the second grade: "It seemed to me . . . I could poke my forefinger through him, and would find inside nothing but a little loose dirt." The bookkeeper who, in the grueling heat, appears in starched collars, white cuffs, and snowy trousers, may look like a hairdresser's dummy, but he elicits Marlow's admiration: "In the great demoralization of the land he kept up his appearance. That's backbone. His starched collars and got-up shirt-fronts were achievements of character."

---

1. the evil spirit to whom the legendary Faust sold his soul

Marlow is also sustained by purely physical work: he finds the labor of refloating the sunken steamer a preservative in the jungle. He is strangely comforted, too, by the unexpected discovery of a manual of seamanship in an abandoned hut up-river. The darkness of Africa embraces both demoralizing savagery and burgeoning life. Along the coast Marlow observes a boat being paddled by blacks: "They had faces like grotesque masks—these chaps; but they had bone, muscle, a wild vitality, an intense energy of movement, that was as natural and true as the surf along their coast."

The Congo had placed Kurtz under too much pressure (as it almost does Marlow) and turned him inside out, releasing the repressed demons of his primitive self. He pursued ivory with the same maniacal frenzy with which Ahab[2] pursued the white whale. In his insatiable ivory-lust, he begins to resemble the object he covets. His bald head looks like an ivory ball and his skin has an ivory hue. His sense of possessiveness has grown omnivorous: "'My Intended, my ivory, my station, my river, my—' everything belonged to him."

Yet he is more than a single European hurling himself at Africa. He is the embodiment of all Europe. The details of his parentage underline this. He is not simply a Belgian: "His mother was half-English, his father was half-French. All Europe contributed to the making of Kurtz." His endowments are the continent's. He is a powerful orator who could have had a great political career had he stayed at home. He was a musician, a journalist, a painter, an explorer—described by a cousin as "a universal genius." Because of these gifts and his final revealing vision, just before he dies, of the horror into which he has fallen, Marlow feels himself in the presence not just of an individual human being but of an immense, almost apocalyptic force.

Like Kurtz, Marlow is tempted by the wilderness. He is aroused by the tom-toms and the barbaric ebullience of the Congolese. He itches to leap ashore "for a howl and a dance." Like other men who have journeyed into the darkness, he feels "the fascination of the abomination." But some mysterious saving element within him acts as a brake—that and the example of Kurtz. By preceding him, by going too far, Kurtz has helped save him, and for that Marlow feels a profound debt. Kurtz has shown him how far he, Marlow,

---

2. in Melville's *Moby Dick*

RECURRING IMAGES ACHIEVE UNITY

The story of a company captain killed in a scuffle over two black hens and the ominous image of two women knitting black wool foreshadow the darkness and danger that Marlow will encounter.

It appears the Company had received news that one of their captains had been killed in a scuffle with the natives. This was my chance, and it made me the more anxious to go. It was only months and months afterwards, when I made the attempt to recover what was left of the body, that I heard the original quarrel arose from a misunderstanding about some hens. Yes, two black hens. Fresleven—that was the fellow's name, a Dane—thought himself wronged somehow in the bargain, so he went ashore and started to hammer the chief of the village with a stick. . . .

• • • • • •

In the outer room the two women knitted black wool feverishly. People were arriving, and the younger one was walking back and forth introducing them. The old one sat on her chair. . . .

Often far away there I thought of these two, guarding the door of Darkness, knitting black wool as for a warm pall, one introducing, introducing continuously to the unknown, the other scrutinizing the cheery and foolish faces with unconcerned old eyes. *Ave!* Old knitter of black wool. *Morituri te salutant.*[1] Not many of those she looked at ever saw her again—not half, by a long way.

1. Hail! Those who are about to die salute you.

Joseph Conrad, *Heart of Darkness.*

can go into the wilderness not just of Africa but of his own hidden self without falling over the precipice or "kicking himself loose from the earth" as Kurtz has. Little wonder that he regards his journey to Africa as "the culminating point of my experience."

After the agent's death, Marlow goes back to Europe and discharges his debt to Kurtz by telling a great lie on his behalf. Lying makes Marlow "miserable and sick, like biting something rotten would do." But the lie he tells Kurtz's fiancée maintains her sentimental image of him intact and thus becomes a preserving falsehood.

At the end we are back inside the protective sheath of civilization, the sheath that guards us against the unbearable pressures of the wilderness and against our own darker selves. Yet as we are once again aboard the *Nellie* with Marlow and his four listeners, anchored in the dark Thames, the final sentence reminds us of where we have been: "The tranquil waterway leading to the uttermost ends of the earth flowed sombre under an overcast sky—seemed to lead into the heart of an immense darkness."

WIDELY VARIED INTERPRETATIONS

The rich text of *Heart of Darkness* has provided critics with a perpetual field-day. One of them sees it as a rewrite of the sixth book of the [Roman poet Virgil's]*Aeneid*, where Aeneas descends into Hades to learn wisdom as part of his preparation for becoming ruler of Rome. Another finds in it the three regions of [Italian poet] Dante's *Inferno*—Limbo: the listeners on the *Nellie* (seamen turned businessmen) and the figures in Brussels; Outer Hell: the bookkeeper, the manager, the ivory hunters; Nether Hell: Kurtz. Still another reads the story as a night journey into the unconscious mind, at once a Freudian exploration of one's earliest self and a Jungian reversion to prehistoric racial memory. Still others interpret it as a retelling of the Grail legend, with Kurtz as Marlow's grail and ivory as the manager's; as a new version of the Garden of Eden, with Kurtz the Adam being expelled from it for having heeded the Devil; as a recapitulation of Freud, with Kurtz as Id, Marlow as Ego, and the manager as Superego; as an account, based on the four references to Marlow in Buddha-like postures, of the arduous spiritual disciplines of Buddhahood.

CONTRASTS AND PARALLELS

Whatever its meanings—the story is complex enough to encompass all these interpretations and more—*Heart of Darkness* abounds in deliberate oppositions. Kurtz is a remarkable man but he is hollow at the core. He goes out to Africa to civilize the natives but winds up his report with a call to "Exterminate all the brutes!" Marlow hates to lie, yet he ends by telling an outrageous one. He is an English seaman who nonetheless resembles Buddha. He is tremendously conscious of how different Africa is from Europe, yet concludes that at bottom blacks and whites are the same. He chides women for leading illusory lives removed from harsh reality, yet when he has a chance to bring the truth to one of them, Kurtz's betrothed, he refuses because "it would have been too dark—too dark altogether."

Darkness and light, Negroes and Caucasians, Africa and Europe, the Congo River coiling and winding like an immense snake and the straight-flowing, tranquil Thames, anchor the story in their recurring contrasts. But even they exchange roles and become their own opposites. Most of the scenes in Africa, the Dark Continent, take place in blazing sunshine, while Marlow narrates the tale back in England at night. The primitive natives, under the pressure of extreme physical hunger, display astonishing restraint, while the civilized Europeans, who come to Africa in search of loot, behave like cruel and barbarous savages. Africa, supposedly backward, turns out to be the place where Kurtz, and after him Marlow, discover ultimate knowledge, while Europe, screened behind the defense mechanisms of civilization, cuts men off from decisive truths. And the Thames, though tranquil, is a "waterway leading to the uttermost ends of the earth," mingling at last with the waters of the Congo and suggesting the theme of the story—the indissoluble and organic oneness of all things that underlies the surface contradictions.

This oneness reverberates throughout. The two black hens in the African village are also the two women in black in Brussels. The grass growing through the ribs of Captain Fresleven slain in the Congo is the same grass growing through the cobblestones of the sepulchral city. The spear that kills him is, figuratively, the same spear that kills the native helmsman who pilots the river-steamer and with whom Marlow feels "a subtle bond." The far-off jungle drums sound to Marlow like the bells of a Christian country. English farmers faced at Dover with an invasion of Congolese would behave exactly as the blacks do when invaded by the Belgians. Analogies and correspondences are as numerous as antitheses and counterpoint.

As a narrative, *Heart of Darkness* has a plot as exciting as any thriller's, and for those who like art to be didactic, it even has a lesson: One must descend into primitive darkness to achieve wisdom, but one must also return to the light. Kurtz descends but fails to return. Marlow makes it there and back, or rather down and up. But in his failure, Kurtz indispensably lights the way for Marlow, and through the power of this great symbolic story of modern literature, he lights it for us as well.

Stylistic Flaws in a Powerful Novel

J.I.M. Stewart

J.I.M. Stewart identifies faults in Conrad's style, but concludes, nonetheless, that Kurtz's Congo symbolizes universal qualities. Stewart maintains that the narrator comments too much, that some of the emotional language is excessive, that Kurtz's deplorable activities are unrevealed, and that the two women characters are superfluous. However, he praises the novel for its dream qualities and its power to convey universal inner darkness. J.I.M. Stewart was a lecturer in English literature at the University of Leeds in Yorkshire, England, at the University of Adelaide in South Australia, and at Oxford University in Oxford, England. He is the author of more than a dozen novels and the critical works, *Eight Modern Writers*, *Rudyard Kipling*, and *Thomas Hardy: A Critical Biography*.

"An Outpost of Progress," one of Conrad's earliest short stories, is about two Europeans left in charge of an isolated and unimportant trading station far up an African river. They are well-meaning men, and when their chief native assistant sells the remainder of their staff into slavery in exchange for some ivory, they are at first horrified and indignant. But their morale has already begun to decline, and they soon acquiesce in the situation and take charge of the elephants' tusks so unscrupulously acquired. . . .

TOO MUCH AUTHORIAL COMMENTARY; TOO LITTLE SHOWING

"Heart of Darkness," in fact, is a reworking of the theme of "An Outpost of Progress," with incomparably enhanced power. Yet, in modified form, the weakness of the first story

---

Excerpted from *Joseph Conrad*, by J.I.M. Stewart (New York: Dodd & Mead, 1968). Copyright 1968 by J.I.M. Stewart. *Endnotes in the original have been omitted in this reprint.*

remains the weakness of the second. In "An Outpost of Progress" too much of the wider significance of the fable is established for us merely in an authorial commentary; what the story "says" is not adequately conveyed as a direct reverberation of the presented facts.

In "Heart of Darkness" the commentary, the evaluation, is, indeed, cunningly withdrawn within the framework of the illusion, since it comes to us from the narrator, Marlow, upon whose emotions—and, one may say, upon the very structure of whose personality—the recounted experiences heavily bear. Yet the result renders the same effect of an inadequate immediacy and precision at crucial points in the enacted scene. Kurtz, whose corruption and disintegration while isolated among savages is the formal centre of the story, comes to us a little too much as an interest, an absorption, a nightmare inside Marlow's head. Consider, for example, how cunningly yet evasively, at the moment at which we feel direct encounter must at last take place, we are offered instead the nameless young Russian in his symbolical harlequin's rags—Kurtz's only disciple, and innocent to the extent of being a kind of Fool Of God. It would be inapposite[1] to expect of Conrad an ocular proof of the fallen Kurtz's "monstrous passions," "inconceivable ceremonies," "unspeakable rites,"[2] and so on; and indeed Marlow himself is nowhere constrained to witness anything of the sort. The most we see—and that at long range, through Marlow's binoculars—is a row of human heads which the respected correspondent of the International Society for the Suppression of Savage Customs has set up to embellish his residence. Perhaps it ought to be enough. Yet the heavily atmospheric and suggestive way of going about the invocation of "things vague, uncontrollable, and repulsive" (to re-quote the earlier story) is often in danger of getting out of hand, so that "the incomprehensible, which is also detestable," is urged upon our attention at once too insistently and too vaguely. As Marlow moves, so he gazes: "deeper and deeper into the heart of darkness." In the circumstances, it would no doubt be unreasonable to expect him to see very much. The trouble is, perhaps, that he seems to gain an obscure emotional satisfaction from the gestures of helplessness he is forced to make. [In *The Great Tradition*,

---

1. inappropriate; irrelevant 2. Critic Stephen A. Reid concludes that Kurtz had become a cannibal.

critic F.R.] Leavis, here sharpening the indictment and turning it upon Conrad himself, says that "he is intent on making a virtue out of not knowing what he means." It is certainly true that portentousness is throughout the main danger hovering over the story. "Heart of Darkness" remains, nevertheless, one of Conrad's greatest things.

THE NARRATIVE IS SIMPLE

The narrative itself is fairly simple. Marlow is appointed to the command of a river-steamer plying between trading stations far up the Congo. . . . The first stages of Marlow's journey acquaint him with the ruthless exploitation of native populations that is going on, and of the utter meanness of its agents. He is the more interested when he hears of Kurtz, a successful trader who has for long been isolated in a remote station, and who is said to possess high ideals and to be a "civilizing genius." The other traders are jealous of Kurtz—so much so that the steamer which Marlow is to take over has been scuttled in order to delay the relieving of Kurtz, who they hope will thus be driven to a breakdown. This has in fact already happened. When Marlow refloats his vessel and gets to Kurtz, it is to find that he has assumed divine attributes and is now mortally ill after for long having indulged himself in unimaginable depravities. He is brought on board the steamer, tries to escape back to his evil courses, is again brought on board, and dies on the voyage down-stream. Marlow later visits in Europe the woman to whom Kurtz has been engaged, and who believes in the unimpaired loftiness of his character. She asks Marlow what had been his last words, and Marlow, although he detests a lie as something holding "a taint of death," declares that Kurtz had died uttering her name. In fact, his last words had been more to the point, for he had cried out "The horror! The horror!" Marlow regards this as having been "an affirmation, a moral victory!" Kurtz at least dies knowing, so to speak, what he has been about. In terms of Catholic theology—although Marlow is unconcerned with this—Kurtz may be imagined as having achieved an act of contrition.

KURTZ CONTRASTED WITH OTHER TRADERS

The portrait of Kurtz, and the enigma of the obscure kinship which Marlow comes to feel with him, derive a large part of their effect from Marlow's contrasting attitude to the other traders. The theatre in which these mean and predatory scoundrels operate is utterly horrifying. Niched in enclaves of supposed civilization "with names like Gran' Bassam, Little Popo; names that seemed to belong to some sordid farce acted in front of a sinister back-cloth"; regardlessly implicated in futilities and cruelties of which we are given vivid glimpses in the French man-of-war "firing into a continent," the chain gang, the Negroes from whom no more labour can be extracted left to die of disease and starvation as if in "the gloomy circle of some Inferno"; seeming to exude "a taint of imbecile rapacity . . . like a whiff from some corpse": the "pilgrims," as Conrad calls them, are utterly despicable in a manner that yet remains finite and comprehensible. They represent everything that is hateful in modern acquisitive society; compared with them, the native crew of the steamer (although cannibals and uncommonly hungry) are models of dignity and self-control. But although Marlow is revolted by them, he is not disturbed. Kurtz, although a "hollow man" just as these are hollow men, is a different matter.

Marlow has voyaged thousands of miles to meet the traders, but Kurtz is found at the end of a further journey— a journey that is "like travelling back to the earliest beginnings of the world." And it is now that Marlow is alerted to a danger against which he has never thought to arm himself; the danger to which Kurtz, "an emissary of pity, and science, and progress, and devil knows what else," will prove to have succumbed. At first it is heard as something in the darkness, far away: "At night sometimes the roll of drums behind the curtain of trees would run up the river and remain sustained faintly, as if hovering in the air high over our heads, till the first break of day." Then it presents itself as a recurrent irruption of a Stone Age, quasi-Dionysiac revel[3]:

> But suddenly, as we struggled round a bend, there would be
> a glimpse of rush walls, of peaked grass-roofs, a burst of
> yells, a whirl of black limbs, a mass of hands clapping, of feet
> stamping, of bodies swaying, of eyes rolling, under the droop
> of heavy and motionless foliage. The steamer toiled along
> slowly on the edge of a black and incomprehensible frenzy.
> The prehistoric man was cursing us, praying to us, welcoming us—who could tell? We were cut off from the comprehension of our surroundings; we glided past like phantoms,
> wondering and secretly appalled, as sane men would be before an enthusiastic outbreak in a madhouse. . . .

3. like the orgiastic, frenzied celebration of the fertility of nature and of Dionysus, the god of wine

It was unearthly, and the men were—No, they were not in-human. Well, you know, that was the worst of it—this suspi-cion of their not being inhuman. It would come slowly to one. They howled and leaped, and spun, and made horrid faces; but what thrilled you was just the thought of their humanity—like yours—the thought of your remote kinship with this wild and passionate uproar. Ugly. Yes, it was ugly enough; but if you were man enough, you would admit to yourself that there was in you just the faintest trace of a response to the terrible frankness of that noise, a dim suspicion of there being a meaning in it which you—you so remote from the night of first ages—could comprehend. . . . You wonder I didn't go ashore for a howl and a dance? Well, no—I didn't. Fine senti-ments, you say? Fine sentiments, be hanged! I had no time.

Marlow, in fact, contrives to witness very little in the way of this savage spectacle—and always from the deck of his steamer, where he has a difficult job on hand. Nevertheless, atavistic[4] impulses stir mysteriously in his heart; he feels the "fascination of the abomination"; is grateful when his civi-lized professional sense finds itself responding to the tat-tered volume he so oddly finds in the wilderness: "*An In-quiry into some Points of Seamanship*, by a man Tower, Towson—some such name." Kurtz, for long held at close quarters with the darkness of native life, has succumbed to it. "The wilderness had patted him on the head . . . it had ca-ressed him, and—lo!—he had withered; it had taken him, loved him, embraced him, got into his veins, consumed his flesh, and sealed his soul to its own by the inconceivable ceremonies of some devilish initiation."

In terms of the surface situation, there is something alto-gether excessive about this, and it may well be that our ac-ceptance of it today is further impaired by a sense that mod-ern anthropology and psychology have to some extent invalidated Conrad's assumptions about "savages" as repre-senting a direct ancestry upon which we may disastrously regress. Conrad is certainly in difficulty with Kurtz's sub-jects or worshippers, and shows on the whole great artistic skill in always arresting them as he does on the margins of his picture: an undergrowth now alive with brown limbs, and now empty; a shower of arrows, feeble yet dangerous; "a cry, a very loud cry, as of infinite desolation"; "the gleam of fires, the throb of drums, the drone of weird incantations."

---

4. traits and behavior returned after a period of absence; like a throwback

AWKWARD PORTRAYAL OF FEMALE CHARACTERS

When he adopts another method, suddenly bringing before us "a wild and gorgeous apparition of a woman" whom we suppose to have been Kurtz's chief companion in his obscure abominations, the effect is rhetorical and unimpressive:

> She must have had the value of several elephant tusks upon her. She was savage and superb, wild-eyed and magnificent; there was something ominous and stately in her deliberate progress. And in the hush that had fallen suddenly upon the whole sorrowful land, the immense wilderness, the colossal body of the fecund and mysterious life seemed to look at her, pensive, as though it had been looking at the image of its own tenebrous and passionate soul.

We feel at once that this woman—although we can, if we want to, give her some conjectural place in Kurtz's story—has no status in the essential fable. Nor has the other woman, Kurtz's "intended," to whom Marlow finally tells his lie. Marlow makes two remarks about women in the course of the book. They are of the misogynist cast in which he is to abound in *Chance.* "It's queer how out of touch with truth women are," he says, early on. And, near the end: "They—the women I mean—are out of it—should be out of it. We must help them to stay in that beautiful world of their own." There is only a very shallow truth in these propositions, however "sheltered" the women in question are conceived of as being. What has got them on to Conrad's page is a kind of inattention—and when we pause on the matter we realize that "Heart of Darkness" is a completely a-sexual work, however dark may be the talk of Kurtz's "gratification of his various lusts." We have to account for the fact that this seems, somehow, all to the good. . . .

KURTZ'S EXCESSES VEILED

[American novelist] Henry James occasionally spoke of "horrors"—meaning gross sexual depravities and deviations on which he was by no means uninformed, but to which he would not have dreamed of granting admission in his novels. Horrors in this sense are, of course, to be posited in "Heart of Darkness." And they remain veiled, shrouded in their proper darkness, no doubt because Conrad knows that this is the most effective way of making a flesh-creeping business of them. Yet they are not *merely* veiled; they are also, as it were, *inert;* and this is because Conrad's imagination is not really much compelled by them. When Kurtz cries out "The horror!" he is not merely acknowledging, at an eleventh hour, the degradation inherent in whatever cruel or libidinous practices we choose to imagine for him. This would not make him the "remarkable man" with "something to say" that Marlow has finally to acclaim in him. When, at the end of the story, some emissary of the Company, wishing to get his hands on certain papers, declares that "Mr. Kurtz's knowledge of unexplored regions must have been necessarily extensive and peculiar," we understand the undesigned reverberation the words carry. Kurtz's evil courses—and this is the final terror of the fable—have brought him to the heart of an impenetrable darkness in which it is yet possible to *see* more than can be seen in daylight by those to whom no such journey has befallen. Kurtz's last words are a statement of the widest generality. They define one tenable view of man's situation in an alien universe. Alternatively, they define the only sense of himself that man can bring back from a wholly inward journey: that into the immense darkness, the unmeaning anarchy, of his own psyche.

THE NOVEL'S DREAMLIKE QUALITIES

It is these further significances—only in the hinterland of Conrad's conscious intentions though they may have been— that largely validate what might otherwise seem disproportioned in Marlow's response to his "pilgrimage amongst hints of nightmares." He calls Kurtz "the nightmare of my choice," and says that in retrospect his whole experience seems like a dream. Conrad was fond of quoting the title of [Spanish dramatist De La Barca] Calderón's play, *La Vida es sueño*.[5] Even so—and as Professor Guerard remarks—Marlow's emphasis on the dreamlike quality of his narrative would be over-insistent were it not that his voyage, in its symbolical aspect, is into a region to which, in general, it is only dreams and mental illnesses that give us access. From the moment that he encounters, in the continental office of the Company, the two ominous old women "guarding the door of Darkness" as they knit black wool, on through the interview with the doctor who mysteriously insists that "the changes take place inside," to the first hypnoidal tremor of far-off drums—"sinking, swelling, a tremor vast, faint; a sound weird, appealing,

5. *Life Is a Dream*

suggestive, and wild—and perhaps with as profound a meaning as the sound of bells in a Christian country"—we are constantly aware of a beckoning across the borders of normal consciousness. The function that Kurtz and his black friends perform in the total fable regarded as a symbolic structure is at least as important in estimating the significance of "Heart of Darkness" as is our sense of the psychological and anthropological "realism" that Conrad achieves. The opening and close of the story on board the yawl in the estuary of the Thames—Marlow's meditation on the darkness which some Roman naval commander must have found here long ago; the concluding vision of the river as still seeming "to lead into the heart of an immense darkness" today—these sombrely-toned termini to "one of Marlow's inconclusive experiences" constitute a simple and superbly executed means of establishing that Kurtz's Congo flows through a darkness we all know.

Religious Allusions in *Heart of Darkness*

Robert Wilson

Robert Wilson claims that characters and events in *Heart of Darkness* represent elements from several religions. For example, he identifies the company's headquarters in the "sepulchral city" with a passage in the New Testament book of Matthew, relates the company clerk to Jove, refers to Marlow as Buddha, and considers the Russian trader a Christ figure. Wilson concludes that Conrad is arguing that whatever religious path is followed, all of them yield the same results. Robert Wilson has researched and written about religion and folklore and mythology in religion.

Conrad wrote two stories on Africa, both of them Christian in tone. The first of these, "An Outpost of Progress," deals with a subject Conrad announced in a letter to Robert Cunninghame Graham: "Fraternity means nothing unless the Cain-Abel business." In "Outpost," Kayerts is Abel and Carlier is Cain. Conrad's account of them is different from the Bible's. . . .

Conrad's second story on Africa, "Heart of Darkness," is concerned with the Christian God in the person of Kurtz. Conrad wrote of it: "It is a story as much as the *Outpost of Progress* was but, so to speak 'takes in' more—is a little wider—is less concentrated upon individuals." Conrad uses Buddhism as a perspective on the influence of God, his value, and the effect the world has on him. The role of Buddha is played by Marlow, whose adventures reveal the history and future of the Christian religion.

Marlow and Kurtz are sponsored by the "International Society for the Supression of Savage Customs," and [in *Youth*]the two men are referred to as "the gang of virtue."

Excerpted from *Conrad's Mythology*, by Robert Wilson (Troy, NY: Whitson Publishing). Copyright © 1987 by Robert Wilson. Reprinted by permission of the author. *Endnotes in the original have been omitted in this reprint.*

Both men are gods endeavoring to bring divine values to earth. Kurtz's report for the Society may be the Bible or part of it. His conclusion, "'Exterminate all the brutes!'" appears to be a summary of the book of Revelation. Marlow also is on "a heavenly mission to civilize" his listeners. Kurtz loses his ideals in the savage wilderness, and Marlow's only hope for appreciation lies with the men aboard the yawl *Nellie.* Marlow's study of the Christian God is carried on through the Buddhist "faculty of meditation." His acquisition of knowledge begins in a sepulchral city where the company headquarters is located. The reference here is to Matthew 23:27, Christ's diatribe against scribes and Pharisees: "ye are like unto whited sepulchres, which indeed appear beautiful outward, but are within full of dead men's bones, and of all uncleanness." The company is in the business of founding religions, and the results are like those described above by Christ. At the headquarters Marlow meets representatives of the Greek religion: the fates in the shapes of two women knitting black wool; and Jove as a Plato-quoting company clerk who knows better than to journey to the wilderness (earth).

The scene of the French ship aimlessly shelling the bush while the crew die with regularity of fever illustrates to Marlow the senseless violence involved in the higher forms of religion. His understanding of Christianity comes through its demonology: a trip up a river that resembles the snake in paradise. Marlow's journey takes him through various circles of [Italian poet] Dante's Inferno. The bands of chained negroes he sees are the Christian faithful who are deathlike and indifferent. At the station, Marlow hears from the accountant (who is apparently working on other parts of the Bible—his account books) of Kurtz's remarkable ability to collect ivory and of his projected success in the Administration of Europe.

CHRISTIAN CORRESPONDENCES

Ivory for Kurtz is like Almayer's gold[1]: it is the valuable ideas that can be reclaimed from the earth. Even the Russian trader, the symbol for Christ, has a small quantity of ivory which Kurtz takes by force. Ivory is the main topic of conversation at the next circle of the Inferno that Marlow visits,

1. a reference to Conrad's novel, *Almayer's Folly* (1895)

THE HARLEQUIN

The Russian trader—the harlequin—with his boyish face is dressed all in motley, his blue, red, and yellow patches carefully stitched on brown. A lone wanderer in the Congo area, he worshipped Kurtz.

The river-bank was clear, and on the waterside I saw a white man under a hat like a cartwheel beckoning persistently with his whole arm. Examining the edge of the forest above and below, I was almost certain I could see movements—human forms gliding here and there. I steamed past prudently, then stopped the engines and let her drift down. The man on the shore began to shout, urging us to land. . . .

As I manœuvred to get alongside, I was asking myself, 'What does this fellow look like?' Suddenly I got it. He looked like a harlequin. His clothes had been made of some stuff that was brown holland probably, but it was covered with patches all over, with bright patches, blue, red, and yellow—patches on the back, patches on the front, patches on elbows, on knees; coloured binding around his jacket, scarlet edging at the bottom of his trousers; and the sunshine made him look extremely gay and wonderfully neat withal, because you could see how beautifully all this patching had been done. A beardless, boyish face, very fair, no features to speak of, nose peeling, little blue eyes, smiles and frowns chasing each other over that open countenance like sunshine and shadow on a wind-swept plain. . . . The harlequin on the bank turned his little pug-nose up to me. 'You English?' he asked, all smiles. 'Are you?' I shouted from the wheel. The smiles vanished, and he shook his head as if sorry for my disappointment. Then he brightened up. . . . His face was like the autumn sky, overcast one moment and bright the next. . . .

Gradually I made out he had run away from school, had gone to sea in a Russian ship; ran away again; served some time in English ships; was now reconciled with the arch-priest. He made a point of that. . . .

It appears he had persuaded a Dutch trading-house on the coast to fit him out with stores and goods, and had started for the interior with a light heart and no more idea of what would happen to him than a baby. He had been wandering about that river for nearly two years alone, cut off from everybody and everything. 'I am not so young as I look. I am twenty-five,' he said.

Joseph Conrad, *Heart of Darkness.*

the region of hell proper (the Central Station) where Satan (the manager) and his cohorts reside. The demons plot to gain as much ivory as possible to insure their dominance in the world. They recognize the assistance that Kurtz provides, but they also are aware of the threat Kurtz poses to them. The Russian trader they mean simply to hang.

Conrad's insistence on the image of "'hanging'" may reflect the controversy during his age over whether Christ was crucified or was executed by hanging in the manner of Attis and Osiris[2] by being tied to a stake. Other descriptions provide additional identification of the Russian trader as Christ. His harlequin costume of many patches indicates his association with a variety of religions. His current alliance is with the Russian orthodox church, and his and the Russian church's use of the Russian language proves unfamiliar to Marlow, Buddhism having no influence in Russia. The Russian trader's adoration of Kurtz amounts to idolatry which Marlow, as an atheist, cannot abide. The Russian's discussions with Kurtz on the subject of love "in general" point to the agreement of Schopenhauer and Nietzsche[3] that love is the keystone of Christianity.

Marlow comes to another circle of savagery, not one of Inferno but the circle around Kurtz's camp formed by stakes with severed heads on them. These heads belong to the heretics and infidels that the Christian Church found necessary to kill to maintain its cause. Such rapacity has become Kurtz's practise since entering the wilderness and coming under its spell. It is a region of Schopenhauer's Will: where undiluted egoism subverts all idealism, even God's. Here the competition for Kurtz is between the native woman, who is the image of the soul of the wilderness, and the Russian trader, the Christ who mitigates and softens God's influence on earth.

KURTZ AND HIS INTENDED

Led by Marlow, another group struggles for Kurtz, and he and the pilgrims try to reintroduce Kurtz to a celestial plane. Kurtz qualifies as one of Conrad's gods because he is around seven feet tall and is frequently associated with thunder and

2. Attis was a solar deity worshipped in Phrygia and Asia Minor; in other versions he was a vegetation god representing death and resurrection. Osiris was an Egyptian god of the underworld, the husband and brother of Isis. 3. Arthur Schopenhauer and Friedrich Nietzsche are German philosophers.

lightning. The god Marlow's group reclaims, though Christian, is dying and then dead. A native announces: "Mistah Kurtz—he dead." (This may be a borrowing by Conrad of a line spoken by a negro in Grant Allen's *In All Shades* (1886): "Him dead, sah, dead—stone dead.") [Poet] T.S. Eliot used Conrad's phrase as an epigraph for "The Hollow Men," and since the Guy Fawkes' epigraph to that poem also represents the slain god tradition, presumably Eliot recognized Kurtz as the dead Christian God.

Even though Kurtz is dead, his influence goes unabated, and Marlow discovers it in painting, poetry, music, journalism, and politics. It is of paramount importance in the continued devotion of the Intended, Kurtz's fiancée, whom [historian and critic Stanley] Renner identifies as the Christian Church. Conrad's use of the word "Intended" may be a pun on the French equivalent *futur* since the girl is as much a time sequence as she is an association. Her black dress and funereal surroundings suggest a phrase of Nietzsche's: "What are these churches now, if they are not the tombs and monuments of God?" To preserve her soul and prevent its madness, Marlow lies to her about Kurtz's last words, but he realizes that his lie is as deadly as the words themselves.

The actual cry of Kurtz, "The horror! The horror!" elevates him in Marlow's opinion to the highest wisdom. Conrad implies that at an extreme point, Christian and Buddhist doctrine concur that the innermost soul of things is an abyss, a thoughtless and cruel nonentity. The story ends with the suggestion that the waterway the *Nellie* is to follow—any path to knowledge—will yield the same results.

Women in *Heart of Darkness*

Jeremy Hawthorn

Jeremy Hawthorn contrasts the Intended and the African woman as part of an analysis of women in *Heart of Darkness*. He argues that idealized European women, represented by the Intended, indirectly support imperialism because they are ignorant of and isolated from the work of the men they support. The African woman, Kurtz's mistress, represents sensuality and passion, a parallel to the mystery and power of the wilderness. According to Hawthorn, Kurtz exploits and ultimately abandons both women. Jeremy Hawthorn teaches modern British literature at the University of Trondheim in Norway. He is the author of *Joseph Conrad: Language and Fictional Self-Consciousness* and *A Glossary of Contemporary Literary Theory*.

It is clear at many points in the text of *Heart of Darkness* that women are given a particular responsibility and function so far as the preserving of idealism is concerned, and at this stage I would like to look more closely at this aspect of the novella's treatment of the relationship between idealism and imperialism. . . .

Three female characters each play an indispensable rôle in *Heart of Darkness*—Marlow's aunt, the 'wild and gorgeous apparition of a woman' the reader presumes is Kurtz's African mistress, and Kurtz's Intended. There is additionally Kurtz's portrait of the blindfolded female, and there are the two women knitting black wool met by Marlow in the Company's office in Europe, women whose resemblance to the Fates of classical mythology is clearly intended. Their appearance in the novella suggests that women may have a significant rôle to play in determining various fates in *Heart of Darkness*. The

Excerpted and adapted from *Joseph Conrad: Narrative Technique and Ideological Commitment*, by Jeremy Hawthorn. Copyright © 1990 by Jeremy Hawthorn. Reprinted by permission of the publisher, Edward Arnold, a division of Hodder & Stoughton, Ltd.

blindfolded woman suggests that this determining influence may not be a knowing or intended one. . . .

THE SYMBOLIC FUNCTION OF MIDDLE-CLASS EUROPEAN WOMEN

What becomes apparent if we consider the three main female characters in the novella, is that in *Heart of Darkness* issues of gender are inextricably intertwined with matters of race and culture. To start with, we should note that the following comments made by Marlow about 'women' are clearly aimed at *European women:* they do not apply to the African woman. Nor do they apply to working-class European women; Marlow's statement is both culture- and class-limited.

> Girl! What? Did I mention a girl? Oh, she is out of it—completely. They—the women I mean—are out of it—should be out of it. We must help them to stay in that beautiful world of their own, lest ours gets worse. Oh, she had to be out of it.

The women are 'out of' the man's world just as effectively as Kurtz's ideas and values are out of the horrific world he constructs in Africa. And just as Kurtz's ideas and values become weakened and impoverished by this isolation, so too do the women who are out of it, imprisoned in their 'beautiful world of their own', end up as debilitated and sterile as the Intended. The remarks quoted above are all of a piece with Marlow's earlier comments about women, comments inspired by his aunt's adoption of the 'rot let loose in print and talk' which leads her to picture him as 'an emissary of light, something like a lower sort of apostle'.

> It's queer how out of touch with truth women are. They live in a world of their own, and there had never been anything like it, and never can be. It is too beautiful altogether, and if they were to set it up it would go to pieces before the first sunset. Some confounded fact we men have been living contentedly with ever since the day of creation would start up and knock the whole thing over.

What Marlow describes as the 'world of their own' of women in the above passage has much in common with the world of Kurtz's ideals, which he does actually try to set up and which does go to pieces before too many sunsets because some 'confounded fact' starts up and knocks the whole thing over. And indeed, just as Marlow's aunt 'got carried off her feet', so too Kurtz 'had kicked himself loose of the earth'.

In a work which, I have argued, explores the fate of an idealism betrayed into a corrupting alliance with imperialism, European women perform an important symbolic function. At the same time as they provide us with a relatively straightforward and realistic depiction of European middle-class women of the time, they also serve a larger representative function, portraying that idealism which the domestic imperialist powers use as apology for their exploitation. This idealism is, paradoxically, nurtured apart from that for which it offers an apology: the activities of the European powers in the subject countries dominated by imperialism. If this argument is accepted, then it must also be accepted that the idealism in question is a weak, emaciated, and unhealthy creature. Neither Marlow's aunt nor Kurtz's Intended could be said to be possessed of any striking features suggestive of energy or practicality. With his aunt Marlow has a last decent cup of tea for many days 'in a room that most soothingly looked just as you would expect a lady's drawing-room to look'. It is one of the functions of women and that idealism which they represent to 'soothe' those off to do imperialism's dirty work. Marlow's patronizing tone when talking of his aunt is however mild in contrast to the powerful connotations of death and disease to be found in the description of the Intended's home.

> The bent gilt legs and back of the furniture shone in indistinct curves. The tall white marble fireplace had a cold and monumental whiteness. A grand piano stood massively in a corner; with dark\ gleams on the flat surfaces like a sombre and polished sarcophagus.

The Intended herself is a thing of black and white, of sickliness and death. She has no energy, no living presence.

> She came forward, all in black, with a pale head, floating towards me in the dusk. . . .

> This fair hair, this pale visage, this pure brow, seemed surrounded by an ashy halo from which the dark eyes looked out at me.

Note how words connotative of idealism such as 'pure' and 'halo' are made to seem unhealthy and corrupted in this description. This seems to me to support the argument that the way in which European women are portrayed in *Heart of Darkness* serves to strengthen the novella's depiction of idealism as weak, unhealthy and corrupted.

COMPLEX BLACK-WHITE IMAGERY

The black-white imagery of *Heart of Darkness*, the effect of which comes to a climax in the meeting between Marlow and the Intended, is complex. An analysis of its function in the passage quoted above would not be easy, and in the novella as a whole it cannot unproblematically be reduced to any schematic system of symbolic meaning. Conrad seems concerned to undercut simple symbolic associations in his use of this imagery, to disabuse the reader of the belief that good and bad can be straightforwardly defined and neatly compartmentalized. Very often in the novella we can observe a process of change from white to black: the centre of Africa is white on the map, but turns out to be a place of darkness; the Intended is pale and fair, but her dark eyes and the darkness falling in her room suggest that her very purity is productive, however unknowingly, of evil. The complexity of this pattern of imagery also seems to me to have something to say about the marriage of trade and idealism in the work: just as we no longer accept the conventional association of white with purity and virtue by the end of the novella, so too we see that idealism can be corrupted by association with evil forces. The challenge to our conventional views at the level of the novella's imagery duplicates and reinforces the challenge made by the work to other conventional views.

It is apparent from the quoted passage that the Intended's capacity is for devotion, not for living. Existence in a world of their own, then, does not seem to produce any sort of enviable life for European women, but more a sort of living death. And inside the white tomb, black decay and corruption can be found. A disembodied idealism, far from preserving the good, may actually foster the bad. If we accept such an interpretation of aspects of the black-white imagery of the novella, we will have to consider critically Marlow's view that if women are kept confined to that 'world of their own' this may help to make our own (that is, the world of men) better.

THE SYMBOLIC FUNCTION OF THE AFRICAN WOMAN

The contrast to the Intended offered by Kurtz's African mistress could not be sharper.

> She walked with measured steps, draped in striped and
> fringed cloths, treading the earth proudly, with a slight jingle
> and flash of barbarous ornaments. She carried her head

high; her hair was done in the shape of a helmet; she had brass leggings to the knee, brass wire gauntlets to the elbow, a crimson spot on her tawny cheek, innumerable necklaces of glass beads on her neck; bizarre things, charms, gifts of witch men, that hung about her, glittered and trembled at every step. She must have had the value of several elephant tusks upon her. She was savage and superb, wild-eyed and magnificent; there was something ominous and stately in her deliberate progress.

Where the Intended is static and passive, she is active and forceful; where the Intended has the odour of death about her, she is the personification of life; where the Intended is a thing of black and white, she is ablaze with colour; where the Intended is refined to the point of etiolation[1], she is 'savage and superb'; and where the Intended is clad in mourning, she is clad for war. Moreover, while the Intended has an air of oppressive sterility about her, Marlow says of the African woman that 'the immense wilderness, the colossal body of the fecund and mysterious life seemed to look at her, pensive, as though it had been looking at the image of its own tenebrous and passionate soul'. This aspect of the contrast is particularly important: the Intended and the idealism she represents are sterile; nothing will come of them but death. But the powerful life of the African woman is, like the wilderness reflected in her, passionate and fecund. . . .

The life of the African woman is all of a piece: there is no division of ideals and aspirations from actuality, no separation between her and her life activity. This being so, the overwhelmingly positive description which the reader is given of her serves as a critique of the life of the Europeans, divided between sterile ideals and brutal 'horror'. I should add, however, that if we look at the two women together we recognize, I think, a familiar pattern: woman as devoted and chaste spirit, and woman as sensual and sexual flesh. But this reproduction of a well-known stereotypical pattern is not itself restricted to the patriarchal ideology that fosters and benefits from it, for in juxtaposing the two women the narrative of *Heart of Darkness* draws attention to the process whereby women are dehumanized by being divided into spirit and body and are denied the full humanity that requires possession of both. . . .

The gender divisions referred to by Marlow are not, of course, just a literary matter, not just a question of the

---

1. sickly paleness; having stunted growth or development

work's symbolic patterns of meaning, nor can they be considered separately from the imperialist brutalities which are recounted in *Heart of Darkness*. The Intended's sterile isolation depicts realistically the separation of those in the domestic culture from full knowledge of what is being done in their name in Africa, while at the same time it is also an accurate portrayal of some of the results of the differential treatment of men and women in the European culture. It is European men who are sent to Africa to further the aims of imperialism; but we see European women—ignorant of what their menfolk are really doing for imperialism—offering powerful ideological support to them. What *Heart of Darkness* suggests to the engaged reader is that the division of ideal and action, of theory and practice, is effected in part by means of the division of genders.

WITH HIS IDEALISM, KURTZ BETRAYS BOTH WOMEN

The African woman in *Heart of Darkness* is one of a number of 'native' women in Conrad's fiction who are betrayed through their love for, or involvement with, a white man. . . . (Both the African woman and the Intended are abandoned by Kurtz, albeit in different ways.) Kurtz's 'pitiless wedding with a shadowy ideal of conduct' is not a happy one, and he apparently finds in the African woman qualities which are lacking in the Intended and which he cannot resist. Kurtz is morally responsible for turning the Intended into a living corpse, and then unable to resist the attraction of a woman possessed of precisely that life which European culture has denied the Intended. . . .

Kurtz manages to destroy both women. As I have said, in different ways, he abandons both. So positive and forceful is the impression given off by the African woman that it is not hard to forget that she too has the word 'tragic' applied to her more than once in the work.

> Her face had a tragic and fierce aspect of wild sorrow and of dumb pain mingled with the fear of some struggling, half-shaped resolve. She stood looking at us without a stir, and like the wilderness itself, with an air of brooding over an inscrutable purpose.

. . . When the steamer leaves, taking Kurtz away from her, we are told that

> Only the barbarous and superb woman did not so much as flinch, and stretched tragically her bare arms after us over the sombre and glittering river.

The gesture is recalled by Marlow later on, during his meeting with Kurtz's Intended.

> She put out her arms as if after a retreating figure, stretching them black and with clasped pale hands across the fading and narrow sheen of the window. Never see him! I saw him clearly enough then. I shall see this eloquent phantom as long as I live, and I shall see her, too, a tragic and familiar Shade, resembling in this gesture another one, tragic also, and bedecked with powerless charms, stretching bare brown arms over the glitter of the infernal stream, the stream of darkness.

The linking together of the two women at this juncture in the narrative makes an important point. Both women are tragic, both have been betrayed by Kurtz. Putting women on a pedestal, cutting them off from reality, and restricting them to a world of sterile ideals and lifeless illusions is as destructive as treating a woman purely as the recipient of passion. . . .

IMPERIALISTS USED FEMALE STEREOTYPES
TO ADVANCE THEIR CAUSE

The Intended's isolation from the reality of Kurtz is a part of imperialism's nurturing of spurious ideals, ideals which function more as camouflage than as active principles or guides to action.

> 'He was a remarkable man,' I said, unsteadily. Then before the appealing fixity of her gaze, that seemed to watch for more words on my lips, I went on, 'It was impossible not to—'
>
> 'Love him,' she finished eagerly, silencing me into an appalled dumbness. 'How true! How true! But when you think that no one knew him so well as I! I had all his noble confidence. I knew him best.'
>
> 'You knew him best,' I repeated. And perhaps she did. But with every word spoken the room was growing darker, and only her forehead, smooth and white, remained illumined by the unextinguishable light of belief and love.

The Intended's forehead seems here to symbolize her unshakeable idealism; unaware of the horror of the world, believing herself to have known Kurtz better than anyone, she is actually more and more isolated, and more and more reduced by her isolation. The whiteness of her forehead parallels Kurtz's own 'ivory' head: unhealthy, unnatural; and illumined by a light. . . .

Why does Marlow remark that perhaps the Intended did know Kurtz best? Is it that she understood his dreams, his ideals, and that these were the true centre of Kurtz, that which could explain both sides of the corrupted idealist? Or is this an indication of Marlow's limitations, of his own desire to maintain a separate world of imagined ideals, a world in which Kurtz's reality would be measured not by his actions but by his expressed values, his disappointed dreams—'a shadow insatiable of splendid appearances, of frightful realities; a shadow darker than the shadow of the night, and draped nobly in the folds of a gorgeous eloquence'? . . .

Heart of Darkness ends with Marlow's decision to maintain the ignorance of the Intended, to keep her in the dark—however much he claims that it 'would have been too dark—too dark altogether' to tell her the truth about Kurtz.

Does this difference represent a change in Conrad's own views about the need to keep women in that 'world of their own' the existence of which makes 'ours' (i.e. men's) a little better? A case could be made for such a judgement, but it seems to me to ignore the fact that it is Marlow rather than Conrad who argues that women should be kept in that 'world of their own' in *Heart of Darkness*. What the novella gives us is not what Conrad the man thought about women, but Conrad's artistic insight into the way in which gender divisions enter into the duplicities of imperialism. I have suggested that the African woman and Kurtz's Intended can be seen as classic examples of female stereotypes: passive virgin and knowing, active woman. The novella suggests that imperialism was able to inherit these stereotypical female rôles and to put them to work for itself, a work that in turn further intensified the domestic oppression of the female sex.

CHAPTER 4

Heart of Darkness in the Context of Africa and Colonialism

READINGS ON
HEART OF DARKNESS

The Politics of Imperialism

Avrom Fleishman

Avrom Fleishman explains the historical effect of imperialism on native people and contends that Conrad's portrayal is objective and accurate. According to Fleishman, imperialism caused warfare among native tribes which broke up their communities and resulted in anarchy. Conrad was particularly irked at the hypocrisy and presumptive attitude of white Europeans. Avrom Fleishman has taught at Johns Hopkins University. He is the author of books on the English historical novel, Jane Austen, and Virginia Woolf, as well as a collection of essays on Victorian and modern fiction.

In Africa as well as in the Indies, the disruptive effects of imperialism on native society were clear to Conrad, and in "Heart of Darkness" he extended his range of perception of social and personal dissolution. The most prominent instance in Conrad's work of a white intruder inciting the natives to deeds worse than those in their repertoire is, of course, Kurtz's provocation of a tribe to organized warfare in order to obtain ivory for export. Contemporary reports of the influence on the natives of the early Belgian traders in the Congo bear out Conrad's account. . . . Even the heads placed around Kurtz's station are no exaggerated image: "twenty-one heads were brought to Stanley Falls, and have been used by Captain Rom as a decoration round a flower-bed in front of his house."[1]

It might still be possible for present-day readers—unwittingly using the argument the Belgian government used to excuse its agents' atrocities—to consider such ter-

---

1. according to the diary of colonist E.J. Glave

Excerpted from *Conrad's Politics: Community and Anarchy in the Fiction of Joseph Conrad*, by Avrom Fleishman, pp. 89–96; © 1967 by The Johns Hopkins Press. Reprinted with permission from the publisher. *Endnotes in the original have been omitted in this reprint.*

rorism as the rule in native life, and to excuse the Europeans as merely entering into recognized modes of warfare to maintain governmental authority. The obvious rejoinder to this was expressed by [American writer] Mark Twain in an outraged satire of the Congo's owner, the Belgian King Leopold: "if a Christian king can perceive a saving moral difference between inventing bloody barbarities, and *imitating them from savages*, for charity's sake let him get what comfort he can out of his confession!". . .

IMPERIALISM CAUSES CHANGES IN BOTH WHITES AND NATIVES

Conrad's African tales, even more than his Asian ones, demonstrate that the contact of Europeans and natives encourages the submerged barbarism of the superficially civilized whites to express itself by genocide. Not only are the natives stirred up by the rapacious policies of the imperialists, but the whites become more savage than the "savages." The process known colloquially as "going native"—already observable in such previous Conrad heroes as Almayer, Willems, and Lingard—is fully realized in Kurtz. The irony in Conrad's portrayal of the return to nature is that it is precisely the most destructive forces in native life which the primitivist acquires, rather than the social values that are also to be found in some native societies.

On the side of the natives, their retrogression to atrocities and warfare is only one effect of imperialism. Perhaps even a more profound disruption is the process of uprooting them from their tribal patterns of life and fitting them—awkwardly and ultimately unsuccessfully—into the patterns of white society. This process has been studied by sociologists and anthropologists under the name of "detribalization," but long before them Conrad had seized upon it as a major charge against imperialism.

The subject has been opened up for literary criticism with the publication of an important article by Harold R. Collins, "Kurtz, the Cannibals, and the Second-Rate Helmsman." Against a background of anthropological information on the distinctions among the native tribes indicated in Conrad's stories, Collins points out the presence of a class of "such 'reclaimed' Africans as the prisoners' guard with the unmilitary bearing and the rascally grin, the manager's boy, who announces Kurtz's death 'with scathing contempt,' and the unstable helmsman, who conducts himself so imprudently during the attack from Kurtz's 'adorers.' The guard, the manager's boy, and the helmsman are what the anthropologists now call 'detribalized natives'; that is, natives alienated from the old tribal life." Collins might have added the fireman on Marlow's riverboat: "He was an improved specimen; he could fire up a vertical boiler. . . . He ought to have been clapping his hands and stamping his feet on the bank, instead of which he was hard at work, a thrall to strange witchcraft, full of improving knowledge." Here the detribalized native is admirably—though inexplicably—following the work ethic, yet Marlow finds his mixture of primitive belief and modern technical ability a grotesque distortion. The implication might be drawn from Marlow's (not necessarily Conrad's) tone that it is better to leave the natives in the jungle than to try to civilize them. Yet it is fair to assume that Conrad could imagine the process of detribalization being accomplished without these human losses.

THE EFFECTS OF DETRIBALIZATION

By breaking up the natives' traditional communities—which provided a provisional security, an ordered life pattern, and limited but realizable expectations—the Belgians opened a Pandora's box from which the troubles of recent date have sprung. It should be noted that detribalization is endemic to imperialism, not merely the result of Belgian policy, although that policy did systematically undermine the tribal authority. The Belgians were doing what seemed prudent to control an enormous territory with a small force. . . . In the Congo, the Belgians needed native laborers in regions far from where they were to be found; they impressed them and transported them to growing cities like Leopoldville and Elizabethville, and thus created an urban proletariat which later became the breeding ground of the nationalist independence movement. They found the tribal chiefs opposed to their appropriations of labor (which undermined chiefly authority) and therefore extirpated them, thus breaking down the tribal structure and the restraining mores that went with it. . . .

The norm against which Conrad's account of detribalization was written is ultimately the concept of the organic state. For Conrad shows that natives, as well as Europeans, are destroyed by the breakdown of their relationship with a stable order of society—by their loss of that sense of identity with a larger reality that gives the otherwise anarchic individual a rule of life. If we were to give a name to Kurtz's vision of "the horror," it might appropriately be *anarchy*: that state of social deconstitution at the opposite pole from organic community. This anarchy is already latent in the individual—individuality and anarchy are implicated in each other—and in the absence of an ordering community it springs into action as terrorism. . . .

[Conrad's] political imagination and the dramatic form in which it is expressed rest on a vision of the ideal society as a genuine community. Measured against this standard, the societies of European nations show themselves to be shabby approximations, but they *do* hold together and give the individual some relief from his anarchic propensities. But in the Congo, in the absence of European civilization and with na tive society falling all too easily into the corruptions imported by the Europeans, that civilization is sorely missed. That is why, in Marlow's ruminations, the modern European state is held up to scorn but its loss is nevertheless considered dangerous. . . .

Conrad's portrayal of imperialism is, then, tied up with a critique of the political communities which engage in it. Making excessive, though comforting, claims on the individuals who compose them, they render men incapable of autonomy outside them. They fail to stimulate internalized moral resources which could govern conduct when police restraint is removed. These societies finally send out to the colonies their least stable elements, their socially mobile adventurers, who run amok in the jungle, destroying themselves as well as the native communities upon which they intrude. . . .

Modern European society is the disease of the communal ideal, a tyranny of public opinion that is even more stultifying than its frequent accompaniment, a police state. Nevertheless, like others in the organicist tradition, Conrad maintains—with all due irony—the ideal of social solidarity despite its distortion in existing states. He accepts the merely negative state at its proper value, while looking toward some better association. This wary acceptance is implied in Marlow's famous description of the English state [in *Youth*]; his listeners live "with solid pavement under your feet, surrounded by kind neighbours ready to cheer you or to fall on you, stepping delicately between the butcher and the policeman, in the holy terror of scandal and gallows and lunatic asylums," and are thereby protected from the experience and vision of Kurtz. But they lack the social values that would place them beyond Kurtz's individualism.

[Critic] Lionel Trilling has noted the "strange and terrible message of ambivalence toward the life of civilization" in "Heart of Darkness" but has placed major emphasis on the appeal of the uncivilized life to overcivilized modern man, as evinced in his perennial retreat from a decadent civilization to a variety of primitive refuges. But for all Conrad's respect for individual noble savages, and despite his suggestion that some village communities were better off without European influence, there is no romanticizing of primitive society to be found in his works. . . .

Professor Trilling is on much firmer ground in observing that the primitive life is attractive just *because* it is ugly. The landscapes described in "Heart of Darkness" are awesomely grotesque (though sometimes dispiritingly vapid). But the implication to be drawn is that European social order, material values, and technical competency are insufficient to the task of beautifying or ordering nature on the scale of the Congo. But the frank acceptance of the limits of human skill generates no love of the intractable medium.

WHITE MAN'S HYPOCRISY AND PRESUMPTION

It is, however, not as much the futility as the hypocrisy of the white-man's-burden claims that seems to irk Conrad. This sense of outrage at presumption, and not merely his mania for keeping things shipshape, charges his satiric account of the chaotic development projects at Matadi in "Heart of Darkness." Not only are the works of imperialism, like the railroad, an insignificant pecking away at the fringes of the African jungle; they do not touch the problem of economic survival in an unbountiful nature, and merely accelerate the collection and export of cash crops like ivory or rubber. This economy fatuity is suggested in the story by the absurd payment of the boatmen in unredeemable copper wire: they have been elevated to a "money" economy, which calmly allows them to starve.

If the jungle is unmanageable as anything but a temporary clearing, do its inhabitants share its awesomely decadent qualities? . . . In an African setting he [Conrad] comes to speculate on the unmotivated restraint of the cannibal crew. Why, Marlow wonders, after being starved and bullied by the Belgians, do they not simply eat them? . . . Human nature remains an enigma, but Conrad succeeds in avoiding the temptation to consider it merely evil or fallen. He elsewhere [in *Rosouo*] lists the virtues of certain native peoples (not omitting to qualify them in the process): "They have kept to this day their love of liberty, their fanatical devotion to their chiefs, their blind fidelity in friendship and hate—all their lawful and unlawful instincts." The human endowment consists, here, of individualism *and* sociality, love *and* aggression, restraint *and* anarchy.

The final vision of Conrad's colonial tales is far from the tradition of the exotic tropics which was still alive in contemporary romantic fiction, particularly in French tales of native passion. For Conrad the jungle, with the people who dwell in it, is simply the wrong ground for Western civilization to choose in a struggle against the darkness. it had better cultivate its own garden rather than try to dispel a miasma.

Colonialism in *Heart of Darkness*

John E. Saveson

John E. Saveson argues that Conrad was influenced by the theories of Eduard von Hartmann in his depiction of Africans and colonialism. According to Saveson, both writers identify the colonial ideal of improving African natives, but show that it failed and instead destroyed lives. With both writers the wilderness represents the primal unconscious, a source of wildness, passion, and darkness. John E. Saveson has taught English at Valparaiso University at Valparaiso, Indiana, at the University of Maryland in College Park, and at Mansfield State College in Mansfield, Pennsylvania. He is the author of numerous articles in journals, including one on Conrad's friends.

Heart of Darkness conveys a suggestion of Eduard von Hartmann's[1] influence more strongly even than *Lord Jim*. The subject matter is drawn from Conrad's own experience in the Congo. Marlow's disillusionment is Conrad's disillusionment. But the tale is invested with philosophical insights so suggestive of Hartmann as to make it unlikely that they were formulated with help only from immediate observation. One striking coincidence is the fact that the same two backward races that stand out in Hartmann's writings stand out also in Conrad's. The Malays excite Hartmann's admiration, but Africans are a degraded people whom no effort can save from extinction.

Heart of Darkness relates the failure of an ethic regarding colonial enterprises subscribed to by company officials known to Marlow's aunt. The "brickmaker of the Central Station" calls them and their appointees such as Kurtz the

---

1. expressed in Eduard von Hartmann's *Philosophy of the Unconscious*

Excerpted from *Joseph Conrad: The Making of a Moralist*, by John E. Saveson (Amsterdam: Rodopi, 1972). Reprinted by permission of the publisher. *Endnotes in the original have been omitted in this reprint.*

"new gang—the gang of virtue." The "cause" requires "higher intelligence, wide sympathies, a singleness of purpose." The unhappy natives are the "reclaimed, the product of the new forces at work." Kurtz is associated with a Society for the Suppression of Savage Customs; to the brickmaker he is an "emissary of pity, and science, and progress"; and his writings give Marlow the impression of an "exotic Immensity ruled by an august Benevolence"—they appeal to "every altruistic sentiment." Conrad here engages a kind of nineteenth-century humanitarianism which he continues to treat antagonistically in *Nostromo, The Secret Agent,* and *Under Western Eyes.* For this reason *Heart of Darkness* has a claim to being called the first of his social and political novels. This ethic differs in no important respect from the ethic of those bemused humanitarians in Hartmann who devote themselves to the improvement of backward races.

The similarity between Conrad and Hartmann thus far is general, but it becomes particular when one realizes that the failure of this ethic in *Heart of Darkness* agrees exactly with an argument in Hartmann. In the statement of Hartmann's theory of the world process, an especially devastating observation is that commercial exploitation is one of the best ways to hasten the extinction of inferior races. Hartmann offers no better illustration of this point than Conrad offers in Marlow's description of the natives in the Grove of Death:

> . . . they were nothing earthly now—nothing but black shadows of disease and starvation, lying confusedly in the greenish gloom. Brought from all the recesses of the coast in all the legality of time contracts, lost in uncongenial surroundings, fed on unfamiliar food, they sickened, became inefficient, and were then allowed to crawl away and rest. These moribund shapes were free as air—and nearly as thin.

On his way to the Grove, Marlow encounters a group of chained criminals carrying baskets of earth from the dynamiting of a cliff.

> All their meagre breasts panted together, the violently dilated nostrils quivered, the eyes stared stonily uphill. They passed me within six inches, without a glance, with that complete, deathlike indifference of unhappy savages. Behind this raw matter one of the reclaimed, the product of the new forces at work, strolled despondently, carrying a rifle by its middle.

The labor of these victims of the European system of law is not useful. "The cliff was not in the way or anything; but this objectless blasting was all the work going on." Marlow almost stumbles into an excavation. "It wasn't a quarry or sandpit, anyhow. It was just a hole. It might have been connected with the philanthropic desire of giving the criminals something to do." The genocidal result—Hartmann's result—of ventures undertaken in the name of universal benevolence is apparent in all these examples. And the kind of irony encountered here, although its sharpness must be due to first-hand observation, in the whole context of the novel has a wryness and philosophical weight very suggestive of Hartmann.

How close the correspondence between Conrad and Hartmann is can be estimated further in certain associational patterns in that part of the text quoted above. The noise of the blasting makes Marlow think of the shelling of the coast by a French man-of-war, which he witnessed earlier. "It was the same kind of ominous voice; but these men could by no stretch of imagination be called enemies. They were called criminals, and the outraged law, like the bursting shells, had come to them, an insoluble mystery from the sea." The shelling at the time strikes Marlow as a piece of "insanity" without visible result or effectiveness. The principle of association in the images and ideas of Marlow's later reminiscence, first of all, is the common end of extermination these forms of "warfare" have and, secondly, is the principle of contrast between the effective and the ineffective. These are peculiar and complex associations and are difficult to explain as anything other than effects of Hartmann's racial theories, especially of his ironic assertion that with respect to the extinction of inferior races, "humane" methods are superior to outright warfare.

One thinks of Hartmann also in connection with Kurtz's abandonment of his humanitarian ideals. At some time during his bizarre activities among the natives, Kurtz writes this postscript to an earlier, visionary report to the International Society for the Suppression of Savage Customs: "Exterminate all the brutes!" This pronouncement must strike the reader as a conversion to a Hartmann-like ethic. Hartmann writes, "The true philanthropist, if he has comprehended the natural law of anthropological evolution, cannot avoid desiring an acceleration of the last convulsions, and laboring for that end." The novel makes much of one other pronouncement by Kurtz, his last words, "The horror. The horror," which are a "judgment upon the adventures of his soul on this earth." Hartmann makes a similar judgment.

THE RELATIONSHIP BETWEEN THE UNCONSCIOUS
AND THE PRIMITIVE MIND

Thus far it has been possible to discuss *Heart of Darkness* in terms of Hartmann's racial theories, as they are related to Hartmann's ethic. It is possible, also, to discuss *Heart of Darkness* in terms of Hartmann's racial theories as they are related to Hartmann's chief metaphysical principle, the fact of the Unconscious. Marlow's voyage from the coastal port to the Inner Station induces in Marlow most of those same insights which turn Kurtz into a pessimist or, in the light of the discussion above, those insights by means of which Hartmann's philanthropist comprehends the "natural law of anthropological evolution." Those insights in Hartmann and in *Heart of Darkness* have to do with the Unconscious as a metaphysical principle and with man in his most primitive and most highly advanced states.

Critics have taken Marlow's journey to be symbolic of an introspection in a Jungian sense[2]; but in Marlow's case, as opposed to Kurtz's, too much has been made of its symbolic character. Marlow's insights are immediate inferences from observed facts; and his journey has often the appearance of a sociological venture. Marlow observes, in the first place, the aspect of prehistoric man; the steamer's progress up the river inspires a "wild and passionate uproar" in the natives on the banks—"They howled and leaped, and spun, and made horrid faces." The Africans on board the steamer in the incongruity of their functions reveal themselves even more strikingly as creatures of irrational impulse. The fireman comprehends his task as a placating of an evil spirit in the boiler—"to look at him was as edifying as seeing a dog in a parody of breeches and feather hat, walking on his hind legs." In the helmsman the sense of duty rests so lightly on ferocious instincts that, during the attack on the steamer, he was "lifting his knees high, stamping his feet, champing his mouth, like a reined-in horse." Introspectively Marlow recognizes in himself the same savage character. He responds to the "howl" and the "dance." By inference and intuition combined Marlow formulates this statement of the atavistic[3] Unconscious: "The mind of man is capable of anything—

---

2. relating to the psychological theories of Carl Jung, especially those that stress the contribution of racial and cultural inheritance to the psychology of an individual 3. traits and behavior returned after a period of absence; like a throwback

because everything is in it, all the past as well as all the future.". . .

THE MEANING AND POWER OF NATURE

A reversion to savagery, however, is not the ultimate danger which besets Marlow and other Europeans. The atavistic is merely an aspect of a more profound psychological change;

PERSONIFICATION OF THE JUNGLE

Conrad describes the vegetation along the Congo in language that personifies it as a gigantic, threatening, mysterious, powerful, and unnerving being reminiscent of the distant past.

The great wall of vegetation, an exuberant and entangled mass of trunks, branches, leaves, boughs, festoons, motionless in the moonlight, was like a rioting invasion of soundless life, a rolling wave of plants, piled up, crested, ready to topple over the creek, to sweep every little man of us out of his little existence. And it moved not. A deadened burst of mighty splashes and snorts reached us from afar, as though an ichthyosaurus had been taking a bath of glitter in the great river. . . .

Going up that river was like travelling back to the earliest beginnings of the world, when vegetation rioted on the earth and the big trees were kings. An empty stream, a great silence, an impenetrable forest. The air was warm, thick, heavy, sluggish. There was no joy in the brilliance of sunshine. The long stretches of the waterway ran on, deserted, into the gloom of overshadowed distances. On silvery sandbanks hippos and alligators sunned themselves side by side. The broadening water flowed through a mob of wooded islands; you lost your way on that river as you would in a desert, and butted all day long against shoals, trying to find the channel, till you thought yourself bewitched and cut off for ever from everything you had known once—somewhere—far away—in another existence perhaps. There were moments when one's past came back to one, as it will sometimes when you have not a moment to spare to yourself; but it came in the shape of an unrestful and noisy dream, remembered with wonder amongst the overwhelming realities of this strange world of plants, and water, and silence. And this stillness of life did not in the least resemble a peace. It was the stillness of an implacable force brooding over an inscrutable intention. It looked at you with a vengeful aspect.

Joseph Conrad, *Heart of Darkness.*

the wilderness awakens in the unwary not only "brutal instincts" but also "monstrous passions." The chain gang by the Grove of Death is not the invention of savages but of "strong, lusty, red eyed devils, that swayed and drove men—men, I tell you." Kurtz is not a savage but a "flabby, pretending, weak-eyed devil of a rapacious and pitiless folly," and he is also a "remarkable" man. In comparison with his abominations, "uncomplicated savagery," to Marlow, is a "positive relief." Marlow's insight, it can be argued, goes beyond apprehension of the atavistic Unconscious to apprehension of something like Hartmann's primal Unconscious. Phrases above seem an elaboration of the evil aspect the primal Unconscious has in Hartmann—"the Unconscious has always something uncomfortably demonic about it." They seem an elaboration also of the capacity for evil Hartmann finds in genius and in the supremely civilized.

Marlow's insight with reference to the primal Unconscious is an inference—with some admixture of introspection—from the progressive alteration of character in Europeans he meets along his route. But, more importantly, it is an inference from his observation of nature. . . .

Centuries of man's toil have transformed the earth into as "sunny an arrangement of small conveniences as the mind of man can conceive," to use a phrase from *Lord Jim*. But its primeval aspect is one not of light but of darkness, not of benevolence but of malevolence. "Monster" concentrates impressions of sun and shadow and rioting vegetation and treacherous reaches into a personification which even in the quoted passage goes beyond literary personification and in the course of the novel is apprehended as a metaphysical entity.

One way in which the novel raises nature to that level is by assigning it attributes. "There was no joy in the brilliance of sunshine." The stillness "did not in the least resemble a peace." It "looked at you with a vengeful aspect." The "high stillness" confronts Europeans "with its ominous patience, waiting for the passing away of a fantastic invasion." Is not the lack of joy and peace in the heart of darkness an intuition like Hartmann's intuition that the existence of the world is an act of blind will "illuminated by no ray of rational intelligence," that the Unconscious feels its existence as a "torment" and a "state to be negated"?

The wilderness has volition. It raises its formidable coast as an obstacle; it waylays the steamer with the hazards of the river. Even though there is a certain amount of metaphor in these descriptions, they are not merely a way of speaking, an effect of Marlow's idiom. Eventually they form part of the novel's statement of Kurtz's relationship with the wilderness; and the most important passages of that statement are not figurative: "it had taken him, loved him, embraced him, got into his veins, consumed his flesh, and sealed his soul to its own by the inconceivable ceremonies of some devilish initiation. He was its spoiled and pampered favourite." The "vengeance" the wilderness takes on Kurtz and other Europeans, presumably for their interference, must be that it makes them instruments of its own dark purpose. Such implications in the novel seem a transliteration of Hartmann's theory of the world process.

The presence Marlow senses and observes, further, is not the darkness of Africa only; it is a universal darkness. England has been one of the "dark places of the earth"— Marlow expands on that theme in the prelude to his tale. The presence is not simply the primal aspect of the earth— that naturalistic explanation will not do, for the presence remains after the earth is transformed into a dominion of light and order. Marlow says that the "stillness" which watched him at his navigational labors, his "monkey tricks," also watches his listeners "performing on your respective tightropes" in England. This is extraordinary logic. One must conclude that in *Heart of Darkness* Nature is as strong a metaphysical principle as can exist in a work of fiction; there is no other conclusion.

Heart of Darkness Questions Popular Beliefs

Allan Hunter

Allan Hunter argues that *Heart of Darkness* is a refutation of commonly believed misinterpretations of evolution and survival of the fittest. He shows that Conrad, by writing a murder story, exposes the cruelty of colonial activities. Allan Hunter has done extensive research in evolution, ethics, anthropology, and literature.

From the point of view of Conrad's use of evolutionary and scientific thinking [*Lord Jim* and *Heart of Darkness*] are the most complex works to discuss in his entire corpus. The reasons for this are quite specific, for Conrad was exploring areas of thought that were in the mainstream of scientific thinking at the time. What is remarkable about the extent of Conrad's debt to other authors is not that he has chosen particularly abstruse areas, but that he bases his arguments on certain extremely well known works and opinions. This thinking, as I shall show, is evidently not only grounded in what would have been regarded as information well-known to every thinking man at the time, but is actually recognisable as a re-writing of certain areas of this. Conrad's rigid empiricism and his sense of his duty to record the facts of his discussion accurately before writing his work, have placed *Heart of Darkness* firmly on *three* levels of reference. First: his own experiences in the *Société Anonyme Belge*, and the growing knowledge that the European public was beginning to receive about the atrocities perpetrated by that particular business organisation; second, his enormous debt to T.H. Huxley's nationally famous public lecture 'Evolution and Ethics', later reprinted many times with equally influ-

Excerpted from *Joseph Conrad and the Ethics of Darwinism*, by Allan Hunter (London: Croom Helm, 1983). Copyright 1983 by Allan Hunter. Reprinted by permission of the publisher. *Endnotes and references in the original have been omitted in this reprint.*

ential prolegomena in 1894; third, his deliberate choice to parallel and even parody the best-selling Rider Haggard novel *She* (1887). There is a very powerful sense that in *Heart of Darkness* Conrad is putting the record right about a large number of what he identifies as popular fallacies.

HEART OF DARKNESS IS A MURDER STORY

Here it is worth making a major point that is nearly always missed in discussions of *Heart of Darkness*, and that is, that this is a murder story. It is, of course, much besides, but there is a distinct and heavy hint that the manager has been busy delaying the relief of Kurtz because he hopes this highly successful trader will die of fever. The hints are clearly there, but carefully muted, and they are worth following up carefully. The excited approach of a 'chap with black moustaches' is the first Marlow discovers of his importance, and he is told his boat has been sunk.

> They had started two days before in a *sudden hurry* up the river with the manager on board, in charge of some volunteer skipper, and before they had been out three hours, they tore the bottom out of her on stones, and she sank near the south bank. (emphasis added)

The sudden panic of both the man with the moustache's explanation, and the manager's decision after such a long wait seem suspicious, and in the light of later circumstances we begin to suspect that the manager has deliberately wrecked the steamer, to hold up Kurtz' relief until he dies of fever. 'The affair was too stupid—when I think of it—to be altogether natural' concludes Marlow. As we shall see, the word 'natural' will begin to have a ghastly resonance. The manager knows that Kurtz is ill, and needs relieving. The manager himself is 'never ill', and the over-riding implication is that if the jungle is ruled by the laws of 'the survival of the fittest', then the manager is 'fit' in a strange inversion of the word, and is welcoming his good fortune, and this concept of what is natural, in order to eliminate his business rivals. Although the plotting is not 'altogether *natural*', it seems to be a vicious extension of the doctrine of Natural Selection that includes murder by neglect. In this light the non-appearance of the rivets necessary for the repair of the steamer takes on a suspicious aspect, especially in view of the following: the manager concludes;

> 'Well, let us say three months before we can make a start. Yes, that ought to do the affair.' I flung out of his tent . . . he was a

chattering idiot. Afterwards I took it back when it was borne in upon me startlingly with what extreme nicety he had estimated the time requisite for the 'affair'.

THE FALSE EXTENSION OF SOCIAL-DARWINISM

It is Marlow's picking up of the word 'affair' here, for the third time, that raises our curiosity, and the implication is unpleasant. The social-Darwinism that has produced the *Société Anonyme Belge* and its rigorous oppression of the negroes, has been extended by the employees into a murderous game amid themselves. Kurtz's success threatens the manager's promotion expectations, and so he must be removed any convenient way. He is less physically 'fit', although ironically the mental attitude that makes him such an impressive ivory gatherer is anything but 'fit'. The manager has re-interpreted [philosopher] Herbert Spencer's famous catch phrase 'the survival of the fittest' (which was often falsely attributed to Darwin by most people to whom the name Darwin *was* evolution) and used it as a law of business. We are faced with the chilling prospect of civilised men, in a jungle, implementing a 'law of the jungle' that is far more vicious than the original article. I say this because much of what was later pushed under the category of social Darwinism was based upon a number of conspicuously false premises. Evolution was held to be synonymous with progress and improvement, whilst a learned body of men, headed by Max Nordau [author of *Degeneration*], put forward the claim that it could equally well mean degeneration. It was not, therefore, biologically inevitable that white men should rule the world because they were quite literally 'higher beings'. In addition, the 'survival of the fittest' did not mean the survival of only one fit individual, as the superlative form of the adjective suggested to so many. According to all genuine evolutionary thought it had to mean the survival of many variants who were fit, *in enough quantity* to ensure another generation. The manager sees the world as narrowing down to him as the supreme being, in a sort of megalomaniacal fantasy, whilst genuine evolutionists would see him as a useful variant only. Furthermore, no matter how nature works, nature is not really in question here, but society, and for this contingency T.H. Huxley had produced a different series of theories, namely that such brutal self-seeking within society was unlikely or 'It may be the destruction of the bonds which hold society together'. Huxley's theories were syntheses of generally established evolutionary attitudes, and widely accepted as orthodox. The whole of the manager's system is a terrifying parody of serious academic investigation, distorted either wilfully or out of blind ignorance into an inhuman code of conduct. Kurtz, starved of supplies with which to trade (we remember the storehouse of calico burns down shortly after Marlow arrives—another plot to prevent him carrying on if he should by chance no longer be ill when contacted?) is quite literally forced to fight for survival, for he presumably faces starvation if unable to barter, and economic privation (the loss of his job and thus of his career) if he is unable to keep up shipments of ivory.

It is evident that part of the nightmare quality of the work unfolds to us only at the level of the omnipotent author. We, with him, see the popular mis-readings of contemporary evolutionary theory. It is ironic that they seem to depend upon punning distortions of words and phrases that are in themselves misleading. As we shall see, Huxley energetically had to re-interpret 'survival of the fittest' publicly since it was becoming obvious that it had been used as an excuse for rapine. The vision Conrad places before us is one in which we see civilised men taking to the jungle what their thinkers have announced as the laws of the jungle—they then re-interpret this amid themselves in the jungle, and what emerges is not only far more vicious than anything nature ever produced, but is defended by them as 'natural'.

This obviously evolutionist bias, taking us back with Marlow into 'primeval' time, is not left there, since Conrad is determined to question and extend the foremost theorists of his day. And he chooses Huxley first.

CONRAD QUESTIONS HUXLEY'S VIEWS

In 1893 T.H. Huxley delivered his famous Romanes lecture paper entitled 'Evolution and Ethics' at Oxford. In it he attempted to explain the emergence of ethics as a living and socially necessary force. He published it, and included it, with explanatory prolegomena in his collected works of 1894. To many, Huxley's articles in *The Nineteenth Century* magazine were the most accessible, and most influential views on evolution of the last decade of the nineteenth century. For the purpose of general publication, the prolegomena were added, in order to explain the lecture more fully to the layman. In

Heart of Darkness we see Conrad taking Huxley to task; the first and most obvious echo is from the opening lines of the prolegomena, which are directly paralleled by Marlow's opening words:

> It may be assumed that, two thousand years ago, before Caesar set foot in Southern Britain, the whole countryside visible from the windows of the room in which I write was in what is called 'a state of nature'.

Compare this to *Heart of Darkness* chapter one, when Marlow starts with a similarly whimsical thought: 'I was thinking of very old times, when Romans first came here, nineteen hundred years ago—the other day . . . darkness was here yesterday'. The difference in intention immediately strikes us. Huxley is interested to point out that a 'state of nature' is a thing of the past that we can contemplate now in safety from the warm side of the window. It is something left, gratefully, far behind us. Marlow places the emphasis on precisely the point that Huxley is anxious to avoid, namely that the separation between savagery and civilisation is in our own case only nineteen centuries—very little indeed on the evolutionary time-scale. Huxley prefers the rather more impressive and hyperbolic ring of 'two thousand years'.

This comparison of pre-Christian Britain and its nineteenth-century counterpart is not an unusual one at this time, since it suggests not only the arrival of civilisation in the form of the Romans, but also the corresponding sense of purpose, and, of course, the arrival of the established religion.

In both works there is a sense of displacement, a feeling that, just as Rome was the centre of the world, from which colonists emanated, now London is the centre and the imperialist urge is similar in magnitude and importance, bringing culture and Christianity. This reciprocating view of history also suggests a degree of inevitability—that just as the Romans had, eventually, to explore Britain and help to raise it to its present status, so the inevitable laws of development mean that this will happen to the Congo, too. The difference is that Marlow reduces Huxley's figure of Caesar to the sketch of a Roman colonist—broke and uncomfortable, 'too much dice, you know', out to mend his fortunes, and this figure immediately brings the description into a different focus. Both passages relate us to savages—Conrad's shows just how small the divide is.

This verbal echo is by no means an outlandish one—none on board the *Nellie* listening to Marlow seem startled by it, either—but in his mouth it begins to take on a more precise, and threatening, aspect. None of the ready-made responses to ancient Rome and classical culture are assumed to exist and taken for granted. Julius Caesar, the great statesman, is no longer a determined conqueror of legendary fame, but a man surrounded by adventurers, in a series of rickety triremes—the same temporal power in whose name Christ was executed. This sort of unpleasant resonance is avoided by Huxley, for he was an established and respectable authority, and as we read further in *Evolution and Ethics* we become aware that he is doing a piece of public relations work for the evolutionists. He tries gallantly to divert our attention away from the several million years of natural and sexual selection in man and his ancestors to the conventional figure of 'Caesar'. He, however, turns out to be little better than a bandit, exercising his superiority as one of the strongest and most ruthless. Huxley avoids this again by his rather homely image of a garden cultivated in a wilderness. To the persuasive quality of this figure of speech is added the assurance that living is no longer Herbert Spencer's idea of 'the survival of the fittest'. In Huxley's view the struggle has changed, and is now concerned not with 'the fittest who got to the very top, but the great body of the moderately fit'. The struggle is now rather gentler, it is 'the struggle . . . for the means of enjoyment'. As we have seen, though, this struggle can be every bit as vicious as the fight to survive, and it is at its fiercest amid the colonists in the Congo trying to gain enough wealth to enjoy Europe. Conrad's vision is in ironic contrast to the following:

> Laws, sanctioned by the combined force of the colony, would restrain the self-assertion of each man within the limits required for the maintenance of peace. In other words the cosmic struggle for existence, as between man and man, would be rigorously suppressed, and selection by its means, would be completely excluded as it is from the garden.

Huxley's image of the garden hardly takes us beyond suburbia, and his reference to 'the colony' when he means a primitive village seems to suggest that he sees colonies as the first, inevitable, step forward by any people—whilst what they are meant to be 'colonising' is, presumably, the jungle they have just emerged from. The linguistic imprecision avoids the most difficult areas of evolutionary thought. Man did not, quite suddenly, swing out of the trees, start building grass huts and cutting down those same trees. The word 'colonise' suggests that a sudden wave of civilisation swept over our primitive forbearers in the same way that the Romans swept over Britain. The two are most certainly not inevitable, natural, or even connected in the way Huxley seems to suggest. Consciously or unconsciously, Huxley takes a great deal for granted.

HUXLEY USES THE "SYMPATHY" ARGUMENT

It should come as no surprise, then, to realise that Huxley all but duplicates Darwin's arguments for the existence of goodwill in Mankind, in what looks like a frantic job to pacify the world at large whilst falsifying science as little as possible. He uses the same argument that man is united by 'sympathy' of feeling, which is bred of a capacity for 'imitation'. This, he asserts, is present in lower animals and is therefore evolutionarily legitimate, and not God-given, especially to man. In humans this has evolved into altruism and a sense of right:

> None but himself can draw or model, none comes near him in the scope, variety and exactness of vocal imitation, none is such a master of gesture, while he seems impelled thus to imitate for the pure pleasure of it . . . By a purely reflex operation of the mind, we take the hue of passion of those who are about us, or it may be the complementary colour. It is not by any conscious 'putting oneself in the place' of a joyful or a suffering person that the state of mind we call sympathy usually arises; indeed, it is often contrary to one's sense of right, and in spite of one's will.

It is evident that Huxley has merely embroidered upon Darwin:

> nor could we check our sympathy, even at the urging of hard reason, without deterioration of the noblest part of our nature.

> The all-important emotion of sympathy is distinct from that of love.

Both sets of statements are rather feeble, and both men use the communal reference 'we' to describe us now, and thus to hint at the impossibility of anyone remaining untouched by sympathy; but this is not the point under discussion, it is the susceptibilities of our distant, savage ancestors that are in question, and whether they would naturally feel the same way is in considerable doubt. Both Huxley and Darwin give us a rather charming picture of humanity, which has evolved itself into a state of sympathy so powerful as to be against its best interests 'contrary to one's sense of right'. Here, we are on interesting ground, since logically too much kindness leads to immorality. Conrad sees this too, but differently. In *Heart of Darkness* what in fact happens is that Marlow finds so little that he can like in his fellow pilgrims that his 'sympathy' extends to the man who is simultaneously their victim and the embodiment of their 'method' of exploitation—Kurtz. And, as we shall see, Marlow does compromise his own morality, for he lies for Kurtz, against his own better impulses. Perhaps this is what is at the centre of the famous image of biting at something rotten—one bites into the best fruit life has to offer, sympathy, and finds that at the centre it is based on a lie, or a misrepresentation. . . .

For the purposes of *Heart of Darkness* it is enough to state that the idea is emerging at a more obviously learned level than the presentation in *The Nigger of the 'Narcissus'*, which stated, as has been noticed by many commentators, the fact of the destructive power of charity, but not the implications behind it. Conrad, there can be little doubt, is deliberately writing against Huxley and Darwin, neither of whom wish to state that this feeling of 'sympathy' may well be rather less noble than they want to admit, and could be defined as enlightened self-interest. . . .

Conrad is illustrating with poignancy, that whatever the learned classes in England were doing, and no matter how enlightened they were, there could be no guarantee either that their doctrines were read, or that they were understood. People like Kurtz, with his desire to suppress savagery, and like Marlow, intent on mending his fortunes, went out to the Congo unprepared. The fact that Conrad chose to use Huxley as an echo is based not only on Huxley's massive influence, but also because in 1893 the Romanes lecture was delivered and in 1894 it was printed, and this is the very time when Conrad was in England still partially convalescent after his voyage to the Congo.

Indirect Methods Convey Conrad's Views of Imperialism

Cedric Watts

In this selection, Cedric Watts analyzes Conrad's attitude toward imperialism. Imperialism is echoed in the story, explains Watts, when the station manager plots against Kurtz's life to avoid being upstaged by Kurtz's success in ivory. Conrad's ironic language also reveals his aversion to racial exploitation and to the corruption and hypocrisy of imperialism. Cedric Watts has taught English at the University of Sussex. He has edited several of Conrad's works for different publishers, is the editor of *Joseph Conrad's Letters to R.B. Cunninghame Graham*, and the author of *Joseph Conrad: A Literary Life*.

When Marlow approaches the Central Station, he expects to take command of a paddle-steamer which will voyage upstream to aid Kurtz. But, on arrival, he finds that the steamer has been wrecked. Looking back on that time, he reflects: 'I did not see the real significance of that wreck at once. I fancy I see it now, but I am not sure—not at all. Certainly the affair was too stupid —when I think of it—to be altogether natural.' The circumstances of the wrecking are peculiar: two days before Marlow's arrival, 'They had started . . . in a sudden hurry up the river with the manager on board, in charge of some volunteer skipper, and before they had been out three hours they tore the bottom out of her on stones.' At Marlow's first interview with him, the manager suggests that the repair will take three months. 'Afterwards . . . it was borne in upon me startlingly with what extreme nicety he had estimated the time requisite. . . .'

The repair is delayed because there are no rivets at the Central Station. There are many rivets at the Outer Station,

Excerpted from *A Preface to Conrad*, by Cedric Watts, 2nd ed. Copyright Longman Group UK Ltd., 1993. Reprinted with permission of Addison Wesley Longman.

but though Marlow requests them they are not delivered. Later we learn that the manager has been in a position to censor the requests.

We gradually infer what Marlow has come to suspect. Before Marlow had arrived at the Central Station, the manager had persuaded 'some volunteer skipper' to steer the vessel on to rocks, and had then impeded the repairs for three months by withholding materials. A further two months are taken by the steamer's eventual journey. By the time relief arrives, the ailing Kurtz, who has thus been isolated for well over a year, is dying.

Conrad succeeds in eating his cake and saving it. The reticently elliptical presentation of this plot enables him to maintain the general atmosphere of futile, pointless activity; while the plot, when we eventually perceive it, makes a bitter comment on the evolutionary doctrine of the 'survival of the fittest' and on the political doctrine that the white man has a moral right to rule in Africa. . . .

CONRAD DESCRIBES THE RESULTS OF IMPERIALISM

'I came upon a boiler wallowing in the grass, then found a path leading up the hill. It turned aside for the boulders, and also for an undersized railway-truck lying there on its back with its wheels in the air. One was off. The thing looked as dead as the carcass of some animal. I came upon more pieces of decaying machinery, a stack of rusty rails. To the left a clump of trees made a shady spot, where dark things seemed to stir feebly. I blinked, the path was steep. A horn tooted to the right, and I saw the black people run. A heavy and dull detonation shook the ground, a puff of smoke came out of the cliff, and that was all. No change appeared on the face of the rock. They were building a railway. The cliff was not in the way of anything; but this objectless blasting was all the work going on.

'A slight clinking behind me made me turn my head. Six black men advanced in single file, toiling up the path. They walked erect and slow, balancing small baskets full of earth on their heads, and the clink kept time with their footsteps. Black rags were wound round their loins, and the short ends behind waggled to and fro like tails. I could see every rib, the joints of their limbs were like knots in a rope; each had an iron collar on his neck, and all were connected together with a chain whose bights swung between them, rhythmically clinking. Another report from the cliff made me think suddenly of that ship of war I had seen firing into a continent. It was the same kind of ominous voice; but these men could by no stretch of imagination be called enemies. They were called criminals, and the outraged law, like the bursting shells, had come to them, an insoluble mystery from the sea. All their meagre breasts panted together, the violently dilated nostrils quivered, the eyes stared stonily up hill. They passed me willilu siv mohoo, without a glance, with that complete, deathlike indifference of unhappy savages. Behind this raw matter one of the reclaimed, the product of the new forces at work, strolled despondently, carrying a rifle by its middle. He had a uniform jacket with one button off, and seeing a white man on the path, hoisted his weapon to his shoulder with alacrity. This was simple prudence, white men being so much alike at a distance that he could not tell who I might be. He was speedily reassured, and with a large, white, rascally grin, and a glance at his charge, seemed to take me into partnership in his exalted trust. After all, I also was a part of the great cause of these high and just proceedings.'

Marlow has been telling his hearers on the yawl *Nellie* about his journey through the Congo some years previously; here he recalls his arrival at the Company's Outer Station. The most obvious and important point to be made about this passage is that it conveys a controlled but intense indignation against racial exploitation and the hypocrisy of the imperialists: there is no doubt of Marlow's sympathy for the exhausted and emaciated blacks of the chain-gang. Conrad had seen actual instances of such ill-treatment during his Congo journey in 1890; and we should not forget that this tale appeared in the year when the Boer War recommenced, with the British and the Afrikaners competing violently for the spoils of Africa. At this time in Britain, the vast majority of Tories, the majority of Liberals, and at least a minority of those who deemed themselves Socialists, were pro-imperialist: the Fabians[1] were, and of course Marx and Engels[2] had seen imperialism as a progressive (though predatory) phase of history. Such bravely humane writings as Conrad's 'Heart of Darkness' and [his friend] Cunninghame Graham's '"Bloody Niggers"' were pioneering works in their forthright condemnations of racial exploitation.

In a lecture of 1975, the Nigerian novelist, Chinua Achebe, alleged that 'Heart of Darkness' revealed Conrad to be 'a bloody racist'. Achebe said that the tale depicts Africans as dehumanised, denied speech, and associated with evil. Africa is seen as 'a foil to Europe . . . , a place of negation . . .

1. Members of the Fabian Society, committed to gradual spreading of Socialist principles 2. Karl Marx and Friedrich Engels collaborated on social theories and wrote *The Communist Manifesto*.

in comparison with which Europe's own state of spiritual grace will be manifest'. Other 'Third World' writers, including Wilson Harris (from Guyana), C.P. Sarvan, Ngugi wa Thiong'o, Lewis Nkosi and Mathew Buyu, subsequently defended the tale, arguing that on the whole its tendency was progressive. Frances B. Singh shrewdly postulated a conflict between the 'historical' and the 'metaphysical' dimensions of the text: 'Historically Marlow would have us feel that the Africans are the innocent victims of the white man's heart of darkness; psychologically and metaphysically he would have us believe that they have the power to turn the white man's heart black.'

CONRAD'S CONTRIBUTIONS TO EXPOSING IMPERIALIST ABUSES

Certainly, some of Marlow's attitudes could, more than seventy years after the tale's publication, seem patronising or misguided. Nevertheless, judged historically in the appropriate context of its times, 'Heart of Darkness' can be seen predominantly as a powerfully anti-imperialist text. There is evidence that it contributed to the international protest-campaign which eventually resulted in the curbing of Belgian excesses in King Leopold's Congo. E.D. Morel, leader of the Congo Reform Association, stated that 'Heart of Darkness' was 'the most powerful thing ever written on the subject'; and Conrad sent encouraging letters to his acquaintance (and Morel's collaborator in the campaign), Roger Casement, who in 1904 published a parliamentary report documenting the atrocities committed by the Belgian administrators. On 21 December 1903, for instance, Conrad wrote to Casement:

> You cannot doubt that I form the warmest wishes for your success. A King, wealthy and unscrupulous, is certainly no mean adversary. . . .
>
> It is an extraordinary thing that the conscience of Europe which seventy years ago has put down the slave trade on humanitarian grounds tolerates the Congo State to day. It is as if the moral clock has been put back many hours. . . .
>
> And the fact remains that . . . there exists in Africa a Congo State, created by the act of European Powers[,] where ruthless, systematic cruelty towards the blacks is the basis of administration. . . .
>
> I do hope we shall meet before you leave. Once more my best wishes go with you on your crusade. Of course You may make any use you like of what I write to you.

The passage from 'Heart of Darkness' quoted at the beginning of this section holds a characteristic ironic contrast. On one side we see instances of the inefficiency, wasteful ness and futility of the imperialists' endeavours—objectless blasting, upturned trucks; and on the other side we see the price in human terms of these activities: the emaciated blacks of the chain-gang, starved slave-labourers. The juxtaposition makes a telling indictment of the folly, hypocrisy and callousness of the so-called emissaries of progress, the 'pilgrims' who, nominally Christians, are idolators before ivory.

However, the passage has greater resonance than this. The rather surrealistic landscape, in which the boiler is wallowing in the grass like a metal animal from another planet, seems to hint of a future time when all man's technology will be annulled by the non-human environment. Similarly, the depiction of the treatment of the Africans implies searching questions: we are led to ask, 'Who are the real "savages" here, the blacks or the Europeans?' This encounter with the chain-gang is just one of the many shocks that Marlow is to experience as he travels deeper into Africa, further towards the Inner Station, deeper into a continent—and into human nature. These shocks oblige him, and the reader, to ask repeatedly, 'What, if anything, justifies imperialism? On what does civilisation rest? And what are the foundations of moral conduct?'

LANGUAGE FORMULATES CONRAD'S THEMES

Another important feature of this passage is its development of the tale's linguistic theme. Clichés are invoked and ironically undercut. After an account of a futile and ugly muddle of machinery, after a pointless explosion, comes the explanation: 'They were building a railway.' We are shown black slaves; and then comes the official jargon: Marlow reports that 'They were called criminals'. In his attention to the uses and abuses, the seductions, ambiguities and limitations of language, Conrad anticipates a major preoccupation of Modernist literature and of twentieth-century philosophy; indeed, the reader of 'Heart of Darkness' will be well prepared for [British philosopher] Ludwig Wittgenstein's demonstrations that 'our language determines our view of reality, because we see things through it'.

Marlow had observed a French ship conducting 'one of their wars' by shelling 'enemies' (i.e. firing shells at the people of Africa); an African degraded by the Europeans is 'one of the reclaimed'; the European 'Workers' (ironically dignified by the capital W) are generally destructive and often slothful; Kurtz's slain victims are 'rebels'; Kurtz's megalomanic depravity is, according to the manager, the 'vigorous action' for which 'the time was not ripe': 'unsound method'. If the Europeans were presented as *consciously* hypocritical, the tale would be less incisive, for conscious hypocrisy entails recognition of the truth. But what Marlow notes around him amongst the Europeans is the credited lie, a sincerity in the use of euphemistic jargon—jargon that sanctions destruction and callousness. Conrad seems prophetic when we consider the proliferation of such political euphemisms in the twentieth century, whether by the Nazis with their 'final solution of the Jewish problem' (i.e. mass murder) or by those tyrannies which conferred on themselves such hypocritical titles as 'People's Republic' or 'Democratic Republic'.

Conrad's attitude to language is janiform [double-sided]: he can see it as truth-revealing or truth-concealing. Marlow strives to convey the truth, though he frequently suggests the inability of language to convey the essential: 'Do you see anything? It seems to me I am trying to tell you a dream—making a vain attempt, because no relation of a dream can convey the dream-sensation. . . .' Kurtz, on the other hand, wields a charismatic eloquence: a power to corrupt others, and himself, through words. Another seemingly prophetic aspect of 'Heart of Darkness' is that through the emphasis on the seductive eloquence of Kurtz, who might have made a successful political leader 'on the popular side', the tale offers a warning against the kind of demagogy that would eventually bring Hitler to power.

CONRAD SUGGESTS COMPLICITY

The art of Conrad is an art of ambush. In his works we see protagonists variously ambushed by circumstances; and his techniques may lead the reader to be ambushed by the text. In the passage cited, we see how Marlow is treated as an accomplice of the exploiters by that African who guards the slaves and who 'with a large, white, rascally grin, and a glance at his charge, seemed to take [Marlow] into partnership in his exalted trust'. After all, Marlow reflects sardonically, 'I also was a part of the great cause of these high and

just proceedings.' The tale concerns complicity. Marlow, as
an employee of the company and even by simply being a European with a European's acceptance of ivory commodities
is involved in the exploitation he detests. The tale's structure
may ambush the reader in modes of imaginative complicity.
The narrative has not one narrator but two. At first, we may
think that the patriotic anonymous narrator speaks with
Conradian authority; but his words are undercut by the
entry of Marlow, with his 'And this also . . . has been one of
the dark places of the earth', and for a while we may be un-
certain of our bearings. Then, as Marlow's narration pre-
dominates, and as we come to terms with his personality, we
tend to accept his authority; so that when he records his fascination by Kurtz we are drawn into a complicated moral
entanglement. Again, Marlow may initially flatter the British
reader by talking of the British empire as an area where you
know that some 'real work' is being done; but Marlow's ensuing narrative, by never explicitly calling the company Belgian or the region the Congo, and by stressing that 'all Europe'—including England—'contributed to the making of
Kurtz', soon dispels the flattery and associates Britain with
exploitation. 'Kurtz had been educated partly in England. . . .
His mother was half-English, his father was half-French.'
The tale portrays a choice of evils: between the thoughtless
corruption of the Europeans who exploit the Africans cal-
lously, and the intense corruption of Kurtz, who becomes a
savage god, adored by the Africans among whom he lives.

Conrad's Racism

Chinua Achebe

Chinua Achebe argues that *Heart of Darkness* is so blatantly racist that it should not be considered art. Achebe maintains that Conrad dehumanizes Africans and portrays the Congo as an uncivilized place in contrast to his civilized England. Achebe sees little hope for improved attitudes as long as Conrad's novel remains prescribed reading in literature courses, and the media continues to marginalize African culture. Chinua Achebe, a Nigerian novelist and short story writer, is the author of *Things Fall Apart, No Longer at Ease, Arrow of God, A Man of the People,* and *Morning Yet on Creation Day.*

Heart of Darkness projects the image of Africa as "the other world," the antithesis of Europe and therefore of civilization, a place where a man's vaunted intelligence and refinement are finally mocked by triumphant bestiality. The book opens on the River Thames, tranquil, resting peacefully "at the decline of day after ages of good service done to the race that peopled its banks." But the actual story takes place on the River Congo, the very antithesis of the Thames. The River Congo is quite decidedly not a River Emeritus. It has rendered no service and enjoys no old-age pension. We are told that "going up that river was like travelling back to the earliest beginning of the world."

Is Conrad saying then that these two rivers are very different, one good, the other bad? Yes, but that is not the real point. What actually worries Conrad is the lurking hint of kinship, of common ancestry. For the Thames, too, "has been one of the dark places of the earth." It conquered its darkness, of course, and is now at peace. But if it were to visit its primordial relative, the Congo, it would run the terrible risk of hearing grotesque, suggestive echoes of its own

Excerpted from Chinua Achebe, "An Image of Africa," *Massachusetts Review,* Winter 1977. Copyright 1978 The Massachusetts Review, Inc. Reprinted with permission.

forgotten darkness, and of falling victim to an avenging re-
crudescence[1] of the mindless frenzy of the first beginnings.
I am not going to waste your time with examples of Conrad's famed evocation of the African atmosphere. In the final
consideration it amounts to no more than a steady, ponderous, fake-ritualistic repetition of two sentences, one about silence and the other about frenzy. An example of the former
is "It was the stillness of an implacable force brooding over
an inscrutable intention" and of the latter, "The steamer
toiled along slowly on the edge of a black and incomprehensible frenzy." Of course, there is a judicious change of
adjective from time to time so that instead of "inscrutable,"
for example, you might have "unspeakable," etc., etc. . . .

When a writer, while pretending to record scenes, incidents and their impact, is in reality engaged in inducing
hypnotic stupor in his readers through a bombardment of
emotive words and other forms of trickery, much more has
to be at stake than stylistic felicity. Generally, normal readers are well armed to detect and resist such underhand activity. But Conrad chose his subject well—one which was
guaranteed not to put him in conflict with the psychological
predisposition of his readers or raise the need for him to
contend with their resistance. He chose the role of purveyor
of comforting myths.

Conrad's Image of Africans

The most interesting and revealing passages in *Heart of
Darkness* are, however, about people. I must quote a long
passage from the middle of the story in which representatives of Europe in a steamer going down the Congo encounter the denizens of Africa:

> We were wanderers on a prehistoric earth, on an earth that
> wore the aspect of an unknown planet. We could have fancied
> ourselves the first of men taking possession of an accursed
> inheritance, to be subdued at the cost of profound anguish
> and of excessive toil. But suddenly, as we struggled round a
> bend, there would be a glimpse of rush walls, of peaked
> grass-roofs, a burst of yells, a whirl of black limbs, a mass of
> hands clapping, of feet stamping, of bodies swaying, of eyes
> rolling, under the droop of heavy and motionless foliage. The
> steamer toiled along slowly on the edge of a black and in-
> comprehensible frenzy. The prehistoric man was cursing us,
> praying to us, welcoming us—who could tell? We were cut off

---

1. return; resumed activity

from the comprehension of our surroundings; we glided past like phantoms, wondering and secretly appalled, as sane men would be before an enthusiastic outbreak in a madhouse. We could not remember because we were travelling in the night of first ages, of those ages that are gone, leaving hardly a sign—and no memories.

The earth seemed unearthly. We are accustomed to look upon the shackled form of a conquered monster, but there— there you could look at a thing monstrous and free. It was unearthly, and the men were—No, they were not inhuman. Well, you know, that was the worst of it—this suspicion of their not being inhuman. It would come slowly to one. They howled and leaped, and spun, and made horrid faces; but what thrilled you was just the thought of your remote kinship with this wild and passionate uproar. Ugly. Yes, it was ugly enough; but if you were man enough you would admit to yourself that there was in you just the faintest trace of a response to the terrible frankness of that noise, a dim suspicion of there being a meaning in it which you—you so remote from the night of first ages—could comprehend.

Herein lies the meaning of *Heart of Darkness* and the fascination it holds over the Western mind: "What thrilled you was just the thought of their humanity—like yours.... Ugly."

Having shown us Africa in the mass, Conrad then zeros in on a specific example, giving us one of his rare descriptions of an African who is not just limbs or rolling eyes:

And between whiles I had to look after the savage who was fireman. He was an improved specimen; he could fire up a vertical boiler. He was there below me, and, upon my word, to look at him was as edifying as seeing a dog in a parody of breeches and a feather hat, walking on his hind legs. A few months of training had done for that really fine chap. He squinted at the steam gauge and at the water gauge with an evident effort of intrepidity—and he had filed his teeth, too, the poor devil, and the wool of his pate shaved into queer patterns, and three ornamental scars on each of his cheeks. He ought to have been clapping his hands and stamping his feet on the bank, instead of which he was hard at work, a thrall to strange witchcraft, full of improving knowledge.

As everybody knows, Conrad is a romantic on the side. He might not exactly admire savages clapping their hands and stamping their feet but they have at least the merit of being in their place, unlike this dog in a parody of breeches. For Conrad, things (and persons) being in their place is of the utmost importance. Towards the end of the story, Conrad lavishes great attention quite unexpectedly on an African woman who has obviously been some kind of mistress to

Mr. Kurtz and now presides (if I may be permitted a little imitation of Conrad) like a formidable mystery over the inexorable imminence of his departure:

> She was savage and superb, wild-eyed and magnificent. . .
> She stood looking at us without a stir and like the wilderness
> itself, with an air of brooding over an inscrutable purpose.

This Amazon is drawn in considerable detail, albeit of a predictable nature, for two reasons. First, she is in her place and so can win Conrad's special brand of approval; and second, she fulfills a structural requirement of the story; she is a savage counterpart to the refined, European woman with whom the story will end:

> She came forward, all in black with a pale head, floating towards me in the dusk. She was in mourning. . . . She took
> both my hands in hers and murmured, "I had heard you
> were coming.". . . She had a mature capacity for fidelity, for
> belief, for suffering.

CONRAD DEPICTS AFRICAN LANGUAGE

The difference in the attitude of the novelist to these two women is conveyed in too many direct and subtle ways to need elaboration. But perhaps the most significant difference is the one implied in the author's bestowal of human expression to the one and the withholding of it from the other. It is clearly not part of Conrad's purpose to confer language on the "rudimentary souls" of Africa. They only "exchanged short grunting phrases" even among themselves but mostly they were too busy with their frenzy. There are two occasions in the book, however, when Conrad departs somewhat from his practice and confers speech, even English speech, on the savages. The first occurs when cannibalism gets the better of them:

> "Catch 'im," he snapped, with a bloodshot widening of his
> eyes and a flash of sharp white teeth—"catch 'im. Give 'im to
> us." "To you, eh?" I asked; "what would you do with them?"
> "Eat 'im!" he said curtly. . . .

The other occasion is the famous announcement:

> Mistah Kurtz—he dead.

At first sight, these instances might be mistaken for unexpected acts of generosity from Conrad. In reality, they constitute some of his best assaults. In the case of the cannibals, the incomprehensible grunts that had thus far served them for speech suddenly proved inadequate for Conrad's pur-

pose of letting the European glimpse the unspeakable crav-
ing in their hearts. Weighing the necessity for consistency in
the portrayal of the dumb brutes against the sensational advantages of securing their conviction by clear, unambiguous
evidence issuing out of their own mouth, Conrad chose the
latter. As for the announcement of Mr. Kurtz's death by the
"insolent black head of the doorway," what better or more
appropriate *finis* could be written to the horror story of that
wayward child of civilization who willfully had given his
soul to the powers of darkness and "taken a high seat
amongst the devils of the land" than the proclamation of his
physical death by the forces he had joined?

MARLOW'S ATTITUDE REFLECTS CONRAD'S ATTITUDE

It might be contended, of course, that the attitude to the African
in *Heart of Darkness* is not Conrad's but that of his fictional narrator, Marlow, and that far from endorsing it Conrad might indeed be holding it up to irony and criticism. Certainly, Conrad
appears to go to considerable pains to set up layers of insulation
between himself and the moral universe of his story. He has, for
example, a narrator behind a narrator. The primary narrator is
Marlow but his account is given to us through the filter of a second, shadowy person. But if Conrad's intention is to draw a *cor-
don sanitaire*² between himself and the moral and psychological
malaise of his narrator, his care seems to me totally wasted because he neglects to hint however subtly or tentatively at an al-
ternative frame of reference by which we may judge the actions
and opinions of his characters. It would not have been beyond
Conrad's power to make that provision if he had thought it necessary. Marlow seems to me to enjoy Conrad's complete confidence—a feeling reinforced by the close similarities between
their careers.

Marlow comes through to us not only as a witness of
truth, but one holding those advanced and humane views
appropriate to the English liberal tradition which required
all Englishmen of decency to be deeply shocked by atrocities
in Bulgaria or the Congo of King Leopold of the Belgians or
wherever. Thus Marlow is able to toss out such bleeding-
heart sentiments as these:

> They were all dying slowly—it was very clear. They were not
> enemies, they were not criminals, they were nothing earthly

2. a barrier designed to prevent an undesirable condition from spreading

now—nothing but black shadows of disease and starvation, lying confusedly in the greenish gloom. Brought from all the recesses of the coast in all the legality of time contracts, lost in uncongenial surroundings, fed on unfamiliar food, they sickened, became inefficient, and were then allowed to crawl away and rest.

The kind of liberalism espoused here by Marlow/Conrad touched all the best minds of the age in England, Europe, and America. It took different forms in the minds of different people but almost always managed to sidestep the ultimate question of equality between white people and black people. . . .

He [Conrad] would not use the word "brother" however qualified; the farthest he would go was "kinship." When Marlow's African helmsman falls down with a spear in his heart he gives his white master one final disquieting look.

And the intimate profundity of that look he gave me when he received his hurt remains to this day in my memory—like a claim of distant kinship affirmed in a supreme moment.

It is important to note that Conrad, careful as ever with his words, is not talking so much about *distant kinship* as about someone *laying a claim* on it. The black man lays a claim on the white man which is well-nigh intolerable. It is the laying of this claim which frightens and at the same time fascinates Conrad, ". . . the thought of their humanity—like yours . . . Ugly."

CONRAD'S RACISM DEHUMANIZES AFRICANS

The point of my observations should be quite clear by now, namely, that Conrad was a bloody racist. That this simple truth is glossed over in criticism of his work is due to the fact that white racism against Africa is such a normal way of thinking that its manifestations go completely undetected. Students of *Heart of Darkness* will often tell you that Conrad is concerned not so much with Africa as with the deterioration of one European mind caused by solitude and sickness. They will point out to you that Conrad is, if anything, less charitable to the Europeans in the story than he is to the natives. A Conrad student told me in Scotland last year that Africa is merely a setting for the disintegration of the mind of Mr. Kurtz.

Which is partly the point: Africa as setting and backdrop which eliminates the African as human factor. Africa as a metaphysical battlefield devoid of all recognizable humanity, into which the wandering European enters at his peril. Of course, there is a preposterous and perverse kind of arrogance in thus reducing Africa to the role of props for the breakup of one petty European mind. But that is not even the point. The real question is the dehumanization of Africa and Africans which this age-long attitude has fostered and continues to foster in the world. And the question is whether a novel which celebrates this dehumanization, which depersonalizes a portion of the human race, can be called a great work of art. My answer is: No, it cannot. I would not call the man an artist, for example, who composes an eloquent instigation to one people to fall upon another and destroy them. No matter how striking his imagery or how beautiful his cadences fall such a man is no more a great artist than another may be called a priest who reads the mass backwards or a physician who poisons his patients. . . .

Last year was the 50th anniversary of Conrad's death. He was born in 1857, the very year in which the first Anglican missionaries were arriving among my own people in Nigeria. It was certainly not his fault that he lived his life at a time when the reputation of the black man was at a particularly low level. But even after due allowances have been made for all the influences of contemporary prejudice on his sensibility, there remains still in Conrad's attitude a residue of antipathy to black people which his peculiar psychology alone can explain. His own account of his first encounter with a black man is very revealing:

> A certain enormous buck nigger encountered in Haiti fixed my conception of blind, furious, unreasoning rage, as manifested in the human animal to the end of my days. Of the nigger I used to dream for years afterwards.

Certainly, Conrad had a problem with niggers. His inordinate love of that word itself should be of interest to psychoanalysts. Sometimes his fixation on blackness is equally interesting as when he gives us this brief description:

> A black figure stood up, strode on long black legs, waving long black arms.

as though we might expect a black figure striding along on black legs to have *white* arms! But so unrelenting is Conrad's obsession. . . .

CONRAD'S LEGACY OVERSHADOWS ARTISTS' DISCOVERIES

Whatever Conrad's problems were, you might say he is now safely dead. Quite true. Unfortunately, his heart of darkness plagues us still. Which is why an offensive and totally deplorable book can be described by a serious scholar as "among the half dozen greatest short novels in the English language," and why it is today perhaps the most commonly prescribed novel in the twentieth-century literature courses in our own English Department here. Indeed the time is long overdue for a hard look at things.

There are two probable grounds on which what I have said so far may be contested. The first is that it is no concern of fiction to please people about whom it is written. I will go along with that. But I am not talking about pleasing people. I am talking about a book which parades in the most vulgar fashion prejudices and insults from which a section of mankind has suffered untold agonies and atrocities in the past and continues to do so in many ways and many places today. I am talking about a story in which the very humanity of black people is called in question. It seems to me totally inconceivable that great art or even good art could possibly reside in such unwholesome surroundings.

Secondly, I may be challenged on the grounds of actuality. Conrad, after all, sailed down the Congo in 1890 when my own father was still a babe in arms, and recorded what he saw. How could I stand up in 1975, fifty years after his death and purport to contradict him? My answer is that as a sensible man I will not accept just any traveller's tales solely on the grounds that I have not made the journey myself. I will not trust the evidence even of a man's very eyes when I suspect them to be as jaundiced as Conrad's. And we also happen to know that Conrad was, in the words of his biographer, Bernard C. Meyer, "notoriously inaccurate in the rendering of his own history."

But more important by far is the abundant testimony about Conrad's savages which we could gather if we were so inclined from other sources and which might lead us to think that these people must have had other occupations besides merging into the evil forest or materializing out of it simply to plague Marlow and his dispirited band. For as it happened, soon after Conrad had written his book an event of far greater consequence was taking place in the art world of Europe. This is how Frank Willett, a British art historian, describes it [in *African Art*]:

> Gaugin had gone to Tahiti, the most extravagant individual act of turning to a non-European culture in the decades immediately before and after 1900, when European artists were

avid for new artistic experiences, but it was only about 1904–05 that African art began to make its distinctive impact. One piece is still identifiable; it is a mask that had been given to Maurice Vlaminck in 1905. He records that Derain was "speechless" and "stunned" when he saw it, bought it from Vlaminck and in turn showed it to Picasso and Matisse, who were also greatly affected by it. Ambroise Vollard then borrowed it and had it cast in bronze. . . The revolution of twentieth century art was under way!

The mask in question was made by other savages living just north of Conrad's River Congo. They have a name, the Fang people, and are without a doubt among the world's greatest masters of the sculptured form. As you might have guessed, the event to which Frank Willett refers marks the beginning of cubism and the infusion of new life into European art that had run completely out of strength.

The point of all this is to suggest that Conrad's picture of the people of the Congo seems grossly inadequate even at the height of their subjection to the ravages of King Leopold's International Association for the Civilization of Central Africa. Travellers with closed minds can tell us little except about themselves. But even those not blinkered, like Conrad, with xenophobia, can be astonishingly blind. . . .

As I said earlier, Conrad did not originate the image of Africa which we find in his book. It was and is the dominant image of Africa in the Western imagination and Conrad merely brought the peculiar gifts of his own mind to bear on it. For reasons which can certainly use close psychological inquiry, the West seems to suffer deep anxieties about the precariousness of its civilization and to have a need for constant reassurance by comparing it with Africa. If Europe, advancing in civilization, could cast a backward glance periodically at Africa trapped in primordial barbarity, it could say with faith and feeling: There go I but for the grace of God. . . . Keep away from Africa, or else! Mr. Kurtz of *Heart of Darkness* should have heeded that warning and the prowling horror in his heart would have kept its place, chained to its lair. But he foolishly exposed himself to the wild irresistible allure of the jungle and lo! the darkness found him out.

STEREOTYPES OF AFRICA CHANGE SLOWLY

In my original conception of this talk I had thought to conclude it nicely on an appropriately positive note in which I would suggest from my privileged position in African and

Western culture some advantages the West might derive from Africa once it rid its mind of old prejudices and began to look at Africa not through a haze of distortions and cheap mystification but quite simply as a continent of people—not angels, but not rudimentary souls either—just people, often highly gifted people and often strikingly successful in their enterprise with life and society. But as I thought more about the stereotype image, about its grip and pervasiveness, about the willful tenacity with which the West holds it to its heart; when I thought of your television and the cinema and newspapers, about books read in schools and out of school, of churches preaching to empty pews about the need to send help to the heathen in Africa, I realized that no easy optimism was possible. And there is something totally wrong in offering bribes to the West in return for its good opinion of Africa. Ultimately, the abandonment of unwholesome thoughts must be its own and only reward. Although I have used the word *willful* a few times in this talk to characterize the West's view of Africa it may well be that what is happening at this stage is more akin to reflex action than calculated malice. Which does not make the situation more, but less, hopeful. Let me give you one last and really minor example of what I mean.

Last November the *Christian Science Monitor* carried an interesting article written by its Education Editor on the serious psychological and learning problems faced by little children who speak one language at home and then go to school where something else is spoken. It was a wide-ranging article taking in Spanish-speaking children in this country, the children of migrant Italian workers in Germany, the quadrilingual phenomenon in Malaysia and so on. And all this while the article speaks unequivocally about *language*. But then out of the blue sky comes this:

> In London there is an enormous immigration of children who speak Indian or Nigerian dialects, or some other native language.

I believe that the introduction of *dialects,* which is technically erroneous in the context, is almost a reflex action caused by an instinctive desire of the writer to downgrade the discussion to the level of Africa and India. And this is quite comparable to Conrad's withholding of language from his rudimentary souls. Language is too grand for these chaps; let's give them dialects. In all this business a lot of violence is inevitably done to words and their meaning. Look at the phrase "native language" in the above excerpt. Surely the only native language possible in London is Cockney English. But our writer obviously means something else—something Indians and Africans speak.

Perhaps a change will come. Perhaps this is the time when it can begin, when the high optimism engendered by the breathtaking achievements of Western science and industry is giving way to doubt and even confusion. There is just the possibility that Western man may begin to look seriously at the achievements of other people. I read in the papers the other day a suggestion that what America needs at this time is somehow to bring back the extended family. And I saw in my mind's eye future African Peace Corps Volunteers coming to help you set up the system.

Seriously, although the work which needs to be done may appear too daunting, I believe that it is not one day too soon to begin. And where better than at a University?

CHRONOLOGY

1856

Crimean War ends; Sigmund Freud born.

1857

Jozef Teodor Konrad Korzeniowski born; Charles Dickens publishes *Little Dorrit.*

1859

Charles Darwin publishes *On the Origin of Species.*

1860

Pony Express runs from Missouri to California; Abraham Lincoln elected president.

1861

Conrad's father, Apollo, arrested in Warsaw; Charles Dickens publishes *Great Expectations;* U.S. Civil War begins.

1862

Conrad accompanies exiled parents to Vologda, Russia.

1865

Death of Eva, Conrad's mother; rapid industrialization in United States; Abraham Lincoln assassinated.

1866

Fyodor Dostoyevsky publishes *Crime and Punishment;* Louisa May Alcott publishes *Little Women.*

1867

United States buys Alaska from Russia for $7.2 million.

1869

Moves to Kraków with father; death of Apollo; Leo Tolstoy publishes *War and Peace;* Suez Canal opened.

1870

Taught by Adam Pulman.

1872

Decides to go to sea.

874

Leaves Poland for Marseilles to become a seaman; employed by Delestang, banker and shipper; passenger on *Mont Blanc* to Martinique in the Caribbean.

1875

Apprentice seaman on *Mont Blanc* to Caribbean.

1876

Serves as steward on *Saint Antoine;* Mark Twain publishes *The Adventures of Tom Sawyer.*

1877

Possibly involved in arms smuggling.

1878

Attempts suicide; enters British merchant navy; sails on *Mavis* for Constantinople; arrives in England for first time at Lowestoft; serves as seaman on *The Skimmer of the Seas* around British Isles.

1879

Serves as seaman on *Duke of Sutherland* to Australia and on *Europa* to Mediterranean; Ibsen publishes *A Doll's House;* Thomas Edison invents lightbulb.

1880

Serves as third mate on *Loch Etive* to Australia.

1881

Serves as second mate on *Palestine* to the Indian Ocean.

1883

Shipwrecked *Palestine* sinks; serves as mate on *Riversdale* to the Indian Ocean.

1884

Serves as second mate on *Narcissus* to Bombay; Mark Twain publishes *The Adventures of Huckleberry Finn.*

1885

Serves as second mate on *Tilkhurst* to Singapore; first skyscraper built in Chicago.

1886

Becomes a naturalized British citizen; certified as a ship's captain.

1887

Serves as first mate on *Highland Forest* to Java; as mate on *Vidar* to Singapore, Borneo; and as mate on *Melita* to Bangkok.

1888

Captain of *Otago* to Sydney, Indian Ocean; first Kodak hand camera developed.

1889

Settles in London; begins writing *Almayer's Folly;* Adolf Hitler born.

1890

Assignment in Belgian Congo; passenger on *Ville de Maceio* to Congo; second in command on SS *Roi des Belges* up Congo River.

1891

Returns to England in January from the Congo; serves as first mate on *Torrens* until 1893; James Naismith invents basketball.

1895

Almayer's Folly published; meets Jessie George; Stephen Crane publishes *The Red Badge of Courage.*

1896

An Outcast of the Islands published; marries Jessie George; moves to Ivy Walls, Stanford-le-Hope, Essex.

1897

The Nigger of the 'Narcissus' published; meets Cunninghame Graham.

1898

Tales of Unrest published; collaboration with Ford Madox Ford; birth of son Borys; moves to Pent Farm, Kent; Spain cedes Guam, Puerto Rico, and the Philippines to the United States for $20 million.

1899

Heart of Darkness serialized; Boer War begins (ends 1902).

1900

Lord Jim published; J.B. Pinker becomes Conrad's agent.

1901

The Inheritors, coauthored with Ford, published; death of Queen Victoria.

1902

Youth: A Narrative, and Two Other Stories and *Typhoon* published; first Rose Bowl football game in United States.

1903

Typhoon and Other Stories published; *Romance,* coauthored with Ford, published; Wright brothers make first successful airplane flight at Kitty Hawk.

1904

Nostromo published; Russo-Japanese War begins (ends 1905).

1905

One Day More, a play, fails; spends four months in Montpellier, France; receives Civil List grant; Einstein publishes special theory of relativity.

1906

The Mirror of the Sea published; birth of son John; spends two months in Montpellier, France.

1907

The Secret Agent published; moves to Someries, Bedfordshire.

1908

A Set of Six published.

1909

Moves to Adington, Kent; Model T Ford first mass-produced in United States.

1910

"The Secret Sharer" published; suffers nervous breakdown; moves to Capel House, Kent; Boy Scouts of America founded.

1911

Under Western Eyes published.

1912

A Personal Record and *Twixt Land and Sea* published; *Titanic* sinks.

1914

Chance published; revisits Poland with family; caught there temporarily by outbreak of war; World War I begins in Europe; Panama Canal opens.

1915

Within the Tides and *Victory* published.

1916

Joins war effort; son Borys fights on French front.

1917

The Shadow-Line published; Russian Revolution; United States enters war.

1918

Borys wounded; armistice ends World War I; Polish republic restored.

1919

The Arrow of Gold published; moves to Oswalds, near Canterbury, Kent; Treaty of Versailles, settlement of World War I.

1920

The Rescue published; League of Nations created; transcontinental airmail begins.

1921

Notes on Life and Letters published; visits Corsica with Jessie; KDKA, Cincinnati, transmits first radio broadcast in United States.

1922

Play adaptation of *The Secret Agent* fails; Union of Soviet Socialist Republics established.

1923

Laughing Anne, a Play published; visits United States; gives reading at the home of railroad magnate Arthur James in New York.

1924

Declines knighthood; dies of heart attack on August 3; buried at Canterbury; *The Nature of a Crime*, coauthored with Ford, published.

1925

Tales of Hearsay and *Suspense* published.

1926

Last Essays published.

1927

Joseph Conrad: Life and Letters, edited by G. Jean-Aubrey, published.

1928

The Sisters, unfinished work written in 1896, published.

FOR FURTHER RESEARCH

ABOUT JOSEPH CONRAD AND HIS WORKS

Gary Adelman, *Heart of Darkness: Search for the Unconscious.* Boston: Twayne, 1987.

Walter Allen, *The English Novel: A Short Critical History.* New York: E.P. Dutton, 1955.

———, *The Short Story in English.* Oxford, U.K.: Clarendon Press, 1981.

Jocelyn Baines, *Joseph Conrad: A Critical Biography.* New York: McGraw-Hill, n.d.

Ted Billy, *Critical Essays on Joseph Conrad.* Boston: G.K. Hall, 1987.

Harold Bloom, gen. ed., *Twentieth-Century British Literature.* Vol. 1 in *The Chelsea House Library of Literary Criticism.* New York: Chelsea House, 1985.

Joseph Conrad, *A Personal Record.* London: J.M. Dent, 1912.

Olivia Cooledge, *Three Lives of Joseph Conrad.* Boston: Houghton Mifflin, 1972.

Frank W. Cushwa, *An Introduction to Conrad.* New York: Odyssey Press, 1933.

David Daiches, *The Novel and the Modern World.* Chicago: University of Chicago Press, 1939.

Ford Madox Ford, *Joseph Conrad: A Personal Remembrance.* New York: Ecco Press, 1924.

Adam Gillon, *Joseph Conrad.* Boston: Twayne, 1982.

Albert Guerard, *Conrad the Novelist.* Cambridge, MA: Harvard University Press, 1958.

Leo Gurko, *The Two Lives of Joseph Conrad.* New York: Thomas Y. Crowell, 1965.

G. Jean-Aubrey, *The Sea Dreamer: A Definitive Biography of Joseph Conrad*. Garden City, NY: Doubleday, 1957.

Frederick R. Karl, *The Contemporary English Novel*. New York: Farrar, Straus & Giroux, 1962.

———, *Joseph Conrad: The Three Lives: A Biography*. New York: Farrar, Straus & Giroux, 1979.

Jeffrey Meyers, *Joseph Conrad: A Biography*. New York: Charles Scribner's Sons, 1991.

Marvin Mudrick, *Conrad: A Collection of Critical Essays*. Englewood Cliffs, NJ: Prentice-Hall, 1966.

Zdzislaw Najder, *Joseph Conrad: A Chronicle*. New Brunswick, NJ: Rutgers University Press, 1984.

William Lyon Phelps, *The Advance of the English Novel*. New York: Dodd, Mead, 1916.

Bertrand Russell, *Portraits from Memory and Other Essays*. New York: Simon and Schuster, 1956.

Daniel R. Schwarz, *Conrad: Almayer's Folly to Under Western Eyes*. Ithaca, NY: Cornell University Press, 1980.

George Stade, ed., *Six Modern British Novelists*. New York: Columbia University Press, 1974.

Ruth M. Stauffer, *Joseph Conrad: His Romantic Realism*. Boston: The Four Seas, 1922.

J.I.M. Stewart, *Eight Modern Writers*. Oxford: Clarendon Press, 1963.

Oliver Warner, *Joseph Conrad*. London: Longmans, Green, 1960.

ABOUT CONRAD'S TIMES

James Truslow Adams, *Empire on the Seven Seas: The British Empire 1784–1939*. New York: Charles Scribner's Sons, 1940.

Arthur Bryant, *Pageant of England 1840–1940*. New York: Harper and Brothers, 1941.

———, *Spirit of England*. London: Collins, 1982.

C.E. Carrington and J. Hampden Jackson, *A History of England*. Cambridge, England: Cambridge University Press, 1945.

Alfred F. Havighurst, *Twentieth-Century Britain.* 2nd ed. New York: Harper and Row, 1962.

Carlton J.H. Hayes and Margareta Faissler, *Modern Times.* New York: Macmillan, 1966.

T.L. Jarman, *A Short History of Twentieth-Century England.* London: Blandford Press, 1963.

Marjorie and C.H.B. Quennell, *A History of Everyday Things in England, 1851–1914.* Vol. 4. London: B.T. Batsford, 1934.

Stephen W. Sears, ed., *The Horizon History of the British Empire.* New York: American Heritage, 1973.

G.M. Trevelyan, *History of England.* Vol. 3. Garden City, NY: Doubleday Anchor, 1926.

R.J. White, *The Horizon Concise History of England.* New York: American Heritage, 1971.

ORGANIZATIONS TO CONTACT

Joseph Conrad Society of America
c/o Professor Raymond Brebach
Drexel University
Department of Humanities
Philadelphia, PA 19104
(215) 895-2446
e-mail: brebach@duvm.ocs.drexel.edu

The society publishes the semiannual newsletter *Joseph Conrad Today*, abstracts of papers, lectures, meeting announcements, and book reviews.

INDEX